# Functions of American English
Teacher's Manual

# Functions of American English

## Communication activities for the classroom

## Teacher's Manual

*Leo Jones*
*C. von Baeyer*

The right of the
University of Cambridge
to print and publish
all kinds of books
was granted by law
in 1534.
The University has printed
and published continuously
since 1584.

**Cambridge University Press**
Cambridge
New York   Port Chester
Melbourne   Sydney

Published by the Press Syndicate of the University of Cambridge
The Pitt Building, Trumpington Street, Cambridge CB2 1RP
32 East 57th Street, New York, NY 10022, USA
10 Stamford Road, Oakleigh, Melbourne 3166, Australia

First published 1983
Fourth printing 1989

Printed in the United States of America

*Library of Congress Cataloging in Publication Data*
Jones, Leo, 1943–
Functions of American English

1. English language – Text-books for foreigners.
2. English language – Conversation and phrase books.
3. Americanisms.   I. von Baeyer, C.   II. Title.
PE1128.J6  1983   428.3'4   82-14716
ISBN 0  521  28528  3 (Student's Book)
ISBN 0  521  28529  1 (Teacher's Manual)
ISBN 0  521  24211  8 (Cassette)

# Contents

# Acknowledgments

*Functions of American English* is based on the British text *Functions of English* by Leo Jones, first published in 1977, then revised in 1981. Thanks to everyone who used and made such helpful comments on the British editions. In particular, thanks to Sue Gosling for her perceptive ideas and encouragement. And many thanks to all those who contributed to this American English adaptation, especially: Michael Sutton, who contributed his great cultural insight, generous encouragement, and much long, hard work; Adrian du Plessis, who made it all happen; Anna Fuerstenberg, without whom there would not be a fine recording; Ellen Shaw, Rhona Johnson, Sandra Graham, and Deborah Menzell who polished and presided over the final stages; and Edwinna von Baeyer, who helped at every stage and found many a lurking inconsistency.

Cover design by Frederick Charles Ltd.
Cover photographs by David Groskind
Book design by Peter Ducker

Cassette production by C. von Baeyer and Anna Fuerstenberg; Speakers: Steven Bush, Sharon Corder, Anna Fuerstenberg, Sandi Ross, Leon Sobieski, Bruce Vavrina; Engineer: David Beare.

# *Introduction to the teacher*

*Functions of American English* is for high intermediate and advanced learners, and is organized on *functional* lines. This introduction outlines the benefits of using a functional approach (sometimes called a *communicative* or *notional* approach) and then describes the way the functional material is organized in this course. Your students will be reading a shortened version of the notes that follow before they begin unit 1. In places where they do not fully understand, you may wish to give them additional information.

## *Who needs* Functions of American English*?*

Most high intermediate and advanced students have spent a lot of time learning basic English grammar and have a good knowledge of everyday vocabulary. But time and again, students have found that knowledge of grammar and vocabulary is not enough to make an effective speaker of English in the world outside the classroom. It is also essential to learn how to *do* things with language – how to use words and structures to do the things we want to do, whether it is to persuade a friend to do something, to describe a machine to a group of people, or whatever.

For students to acquire this *communicative competence* they must learn more than just grammar and vocabulary. They must learn which structures are *appropriate* to the situation they are in and the people they are with. They must learn to use a range of expressions (some of which they already know, some of which are new) that are commonly used to agree, to complain, to discuss the future, and so on. They must learn to conduct conversations – beginnings, middles, and endings – that are fluent and natural.

The functional approach provides a means of organizing all the material that must be mastered before a person can be said to have "learned a language." The approach involves isolating certain *language functions*, such as "asking for information" (unit 2), "refusing to do something" (unit 3), "giving an opinion" (unit 8), and so on. These functions are then learned by practicing them in a variety of everyday situations. Each situation involves common *roles* (friend, stranger, employee, customer), typical *settings* (on a plane, at a party, at a meeting), and likely *topics* (business, travel, sport).

The emphasis is on developing *fluency* – giving students lots of practice in dealing with frequently encountered functions and situations. Any student who intends to *use* the language can benefit.

## What good is the functional approach?

The functional approach does not *replace* traditional language teaching – it adds a new dimension to it. Grammar and vocabulary must still be learned – students must know how to use future verb forms before they can talk about the future in true-to-life situations that involve making predictions and stating intentions (as in unit 6). In addition, grammar and vocabulary should certainly be reviewed in the usual way when their use in activities shows that they have not been mastered. But grammar and vocabulary are now simply the *tools* needed to communicate naturally in speaking and in writing. The aim is clearly communication – first in class and then outside it.

The specific goal of this approach is to get students in class to engage in communication that is as close as possible to the "real thing." This goal is achieved by special emphasis on two principles:

– Students must be involved in as many situations as possible where one of them has some information and another one doesn't but has to get it. Such situations are said to contain an *information gap* between the participants – in the traditional classroom situation, students are often told information that they already know, and this is not realistic. The communication activities (described on p. 8) were specially designed to create such information gaps.
– Students must be involved in as many situations as possible where they must *choose* from a variety of expressions. Several different ways of putting a function into words must be learned – there is never just one way of achieving a goal with language. Students may settle on favorite expressions, but they must also understand many different ways of expressing a particular function. The lists of expressions in the presentation sections in every unit (described later) provide many opportunitites for such choices by the students.

## What does the teacher do in Functions of American English?

The materials encourage a very active approach to language practice. There are many different types of exercises and activities that stimulate a lot of talking and will often be amusing. These will increase the confidence of students and improve their accuracy in conversation. Students are often asked to play different roles, and it is only fair that you the teacher should sometimes join in. Playing a role does not demand any acting skill or funny clothes and voices – it just requires setting the scene carefully to make the situation believable.

As with any textbook, you will find that there are things you want to leave out and things you want to put in – any adaptation of the material to suit the needs and interests of your class will make the book more functional! The questionnaire in unit 1 is a good starting point for finding out from your students what their needs, interests, and expectations really are.

*Functions of American English* will help improve students' listening, speaking, and writing skills, but your class may need further work in reading as well as supplementary work in listening comprehension. Such extra material is best chosen by the individual teacher to suit the needs and interests of the class.

## Organization of the materials

### Overall plan

The Student's Book and Teacher's Manual each consists of an introduction and fifteen units – the Student's Book contains the lesson material and 153 communication activities, and the Teacher's Manual contains teacher's notes with additional suggestions. The numbering of sections in the two books is the same for easy reference. A cassette tape completes the course material – it contains all the conversations, presentations, and pattern conversations. (These sections are identified by the sign ▣ in the Student's Book and Teacher's Manual.)

### Length of the course

Each of the fifteen units might take three to four periods of 45–50 minutes each to cover. So the whole course could be completed in forty-five to sixty periods, depending on how much extra time is spent on such things as the sections of most interest to the class, remedial language work, and the written work sections. Students are encouraged to ask for more (or less) time on activities they feel are more (or less) relevant to their needs.

It is recommended that work with *Functions of American English* be interspersed with work on other sorts of materials appropriate to your students' needs, such as additional grammar and vocabulary as well as reading and listening materials.

### Format of each unit

Each unit in the two books is divided into several sections:

---

#### Unit title
The title of each unit consists of the major functions that are focused on. There are usually three of them (see Contents).

#### Functional objectives (only in Teacher's Manual)
A short statement is given of the abilities that students will focus on in that unit. These objectives should be outlined to your students before the unit is done in terms that they can relate to – by referring to their own jobs, interests, and needs, for example. It is also essential to assess the achievement of these objectives while working on a unit and to ask the students if they feel they have achieved them by the end of the unit. A simple question like *What do you think you've learned from this unit?* might be a suitable way of finding out.

#### Presupposed knowledge (only in Teacher's Manual)
Not every unit has a presupposed knowledge section, but where there is one it gives a brief list of essential grammatical structures needed to perform the language functions in that unit. If a short assessment of your students' knowledge shows that they cannot use these structures, they will need preliminary review and practice before starting the unit, perhaps a book like:

Danielson, D. & R. Hayden. *Using English: Your Second Language.* Englewood Cliffs, N.J.: Prentice-Hall, 1973.

Frank, Marcella. *Modern English: A Practical Reference Guide* and *Exercises for Non-Native Speakers (Part I – Parts of Speech* and *Part II – Sentences and Complex Structures).* Englewood Cliffs, N.J.: Prentice-Hall, 1972.

Krohn, Robert. *English Sentence Structure.* Ann Arbor: University of Michigan Press, 1971.

Rutherford, William. *Modern English, Vols. 1 and 2.* New York: Harcourt Brace Jovanovich, 1975.

For teachers who do not mind adapting materials from British English texts, the following two texts have grammar exercises suitable for use with *Functions of American English*:

Jones, Leo. *Notions in English.* Cambridge: Cambridge University Press, 1979.

O'Neill, R. *English in Situations.* Oxford: Oxford University Press, 1970.

---

## Conversation

*Content*

Each unit begins with a conversation that was recorded in everyday language, with all its hesitations and false starts. This is *not* a "dialogue" that the student should memorize. The conversation presents a performance in a typical situation of the functions focused on in the unit. In this way, students are introduced to some of the expressions that are used to carry out the functions, and they can see how the expressions are used by native speakers of English in a real conversation.

The situations involve two or three people at a time. The same six characters keep appearing in the situations, so the class will become familiar with them as real people:

Bob and Mary Graham – He works in an office, she at home.
John Spencer – He installs telephones but can't cook.
Anne Kennedy – She works in a trust company and likes John.
Sue Brown – She does photography and doesn't like violence on TV.
Ken Davis – He drives a big car and likes to smoke.

*Procedure*

A good way to use the conversations on tape is as follows:
1 Describe to the students the characters and the situation they are in, as given in the teacher's notes for each conversation. Play the entire conversation once or twice, and then ask general comprehension and summary questions. In later units, you may want to have the students guess the characters and situation after the first play-through, instead of telling them this information at the beginning. Discuss the relationship between the speakers.

2 Play the conversation, stopping it frequently before a speaker has finished, and ask: *What's he or she going to say next?* This will help to train students to *predict* or *anticipate* what people are going to say – an essential skill in understanding spoken English.

3 Play the conversation and ask the students to spot examples of the language functions being performed. Get them to mark these in their books. Discuss the effect of each example on the listener.

4 Discuss with the class any observations or problems arising from the conversation.

*Giving more examples*

The conversations can display only a few of the expressions that are presented in each unit, so you may have to give additional examples of your own to demonstrate the use of other expressions that you decide to present later on (see description of presentation sections that follows).

*Variety*

It is a good idea to use a variety of procedures with the conversations. Play a conversation section at the *end* of a unit occasionally. Concentrate more on step 2 (above) in one unit, more on step 3 in another. Sometimes use the alternative ideas suggested in the teacher's notes on each conversation.

*Teacher's notes*

The teacher's notes give the characters, situation, and topic(s) of each conversation, as well as alternative ideas for introducing each unit. The first three conversations are reproduced in the form of an annotated transcript, with the functions labeled and the expressions that are used to carry out the functions in italics.

---

## Presentations

*Content*

The presentation sections include descriptions of the functions and various ways of carrying them out. Each unit usually has three presentation sections, each followed by various exercises and activities. One presentation section and its exercises might take about 45–60 minutes of class time to cover.

*Procedure*

Students should be asked to read these sections by themselves, preferably at home, before you cover them in class. A good way to handle the presentation sections is to have the students close their books and for you to use the tape and a blackboard. The tape presents expressions used to carry out the function under discussion in a lively way, and you can then provide further information and personal advice on how and when to use them correctly.

Alternatively, provided your class has thoroughly prepared itself for work on this section beforehand, you can call on the students to remember expressions, so that ideas will come from them – it is always better for students to make suggestions than for the teacher to "spoonfeed" them.

Whichever procedure you use, allow your students to introduce similar expressions from their own experience. Ask them to suggest examples of each expression in use. Make sure they can decide when each expression would be appropriate.

*Changing the expressions*

You are encouraged to change the lists of expressions that are provided in the presentation sections to suit your own or the local way of speaking. You should feel free to add, drop, or modify expressions. (If you are not sure about the appropriateness of an expression ask a native speaker about it.) In any case, you may decide to concentrate your teaching on a selection of expressions that is not too easy or too hard for your class.

| | |
|---|---|
| *Choice of expressions* | From the set of expressions that you cover in class – there should always be several for each function – your students should be free to choose a few as their own favorites. The focus of each lesson should be on *understanding* functions expressed in a *wide* variety of ways, but *expressing* functions in a *few* ways that the students feel most comfortable with. This element of choosing some expressions from a possible range is precisely what fluent speakers of a language do all the time – we know more expressions than we use, and we must always make a quick choice of one expression to use in any given situation. This is an essential ingredient of the functional approach. |
| *Unpredict-able language* | Some of the essential information is not given in the presentation section at all – often the most important thing is what students say *after* an introductory phrase. But since no once can predict what a student will actually say after *As I see it . . .* , for example, this information cannot be given in the book. Whatever students say, you must be prepared to provide some necessary vocabulary, to offer advice on usage, and to correct mistakes. True communication, which is the goal at this level of language learning, is often expressed through language that is unpredictable. Although dealing with this sort of unpredictable language may seem very demanding, it is certainly also extremely rewarding, and it is an essential part of training students to actually communicate their ideas. |
| *Pronuncia-tion and simple drills* | It may be necessary for you to do some controlled pronunciation practice – the tape will be useful for this. Students have to feel comfortable pronouncing an expression, especially if it's a long one, before they can start to use it. Pay particular attention to the tone of voice, for example, the polite and impolite way of saying *Would you open the window, please?* Apart from repetition of the new expressions in short sentences, your class may also benefit from some simple drills of the recommended expressions before moving on to the other exercises. In these simple drills, students need not produce complete, accurate communications but should use the recommended expressions in brief exchanges. Ideas for several such drills will be found in the presentation sections in the teacher's notes. |
| *Teacher's notes* | Additional expressions that you may want to teach are given. There are also notes on points to watch out for and suggestions for some simple drills of the expressions being taught. |

## Exercises

There are three different kinds of exercise sections for practicing the material taught in the presentation sections. An exercise can take anywhere from 10 to 25 minutes to do.

| | |
|---|---|
| *Teacher-controlled exercises* | The first exercise after each presentation is usually "teacher controlled," so that you have a chance to advise and correct your class before the freer exercise sections. Try to concentrate on helping the students to express themselves. Encourage them not to play safe but to experiment. Help them |

to concentrate on using the recommended expressions. Encourage them to use some "new" expressions rather than just the "easy" expressions they know already. You may need to interrupt frequently during this first exercise section.

*Freer exercises*

The later exercise sections are much freer. They are designed to build confidence and fluency. Many of these sections require students to work together in pairs or small groups. It is important to set the scene very carefully in many of these exercises so that the students know exactly what they have to do and can get involved in the situation. Such scene-setting comes to life more if you do it in your own personal way, rather than relying on the printed words in the book.

*Consolidation exercises*

Finally, many units have a consolidation exercise at the end that practices expressions from all the presentations in the unit.

*Procedures:*

*Monitoring students' performance*

In the freer exercises, it is important not to interrupt students in the middle of a sentence or conversation just because a mistake has been made. This does not mean that you can sit back and relax – you should go around the room *monitoring* the conversations. This involves making notes of some good, and some not-so-good, ways of expressing oneself that you hear (these will be used later). Help students who are stuck, but try not to give too much help – otherwise the students will come to rely on you constantly. And don't correct every mistake – otherwise the students may become too mistake-conscious and tongue-tied. You will find the students correcting each other as they get used to such exercises, and this can be very effective if it is not overdone. Make sure you pause for questions after each exercise; this lets the students air their difficulties and gives you a chance to discuss what you heard as you went around the room.

*Repeating exercises*

You may find the students had so much trouble with a particular exercise that you want to do it all over again, perhaps in different groups. This kind of "replay" can increase confidence a lot and provide a tangible feeling of sudden progress that is often lacking at this level of language learning and that students often find reassuring.

*The extra student*

One minor problem in pair work is that in a class with an odd number of students, one person is left over after the rest of the class has paired off. This is easily solved by having the extra student share the work of one member of a pair. Suggestions for working with an extra student are given where necessary in the teacher's notes.

*Changing partners*

Do not allow students to talk to the same partner every time. Rearrange seating regularly or make sure that students change partners frequently. This will make conversations less predictable, and so more realistic. It will also make the exercises more interesting and lively – students can easily get bored with a regular partner.

*Recording and performing*

Once in a while, if possible, record a group in action (using audio or even video) and play back the recording for analysis by the rest of the class. From time to time ask a group to "perform" in front of the class after they have "rehearsed" their conversation.

| | |
|---|---|
| *Benefits of group work* | The rationale behind pair or group work may need to be explained to students who feel that they should be corrected constantly by the teacher or that the teacher should control the whole lesson. Reasons for using pair and group work in this course include the following: |
| | The amount of student talking time is greatly increased, and the more students talk, the more fluent they become. |
| | Students feel less inhibited when talking privately to another student than when talking in front of the whole class. When they are less inhibited, they experiment more and discover how much they can actually communicate using the English they know already. |
| | Playing roles in the exercises prepares students in a non-threatening way for the roles they may need to play in real-life situations in English. |
| *Teacher's notes* | Additional ideas for teacher-controlled exercises are given, as well as additional ideas for freer exercises. |

## Communication activities

| | |
|---|---|
| *Content* | The freest, most open-ended exercises of all are the communication activities. These involve two or more sides communicating with each other in discussions, role plays, problem-solving activities, and so on. |
| *Format* | The communication activity sections in the individual units give instructions on (a) how to divide up the class, (b) the subject of the activity, and (c) with what activity number to begin in the *Communication activities* section at the back of the book. One activity at the back of the book often leads to another, until the students are instructed to reassemble as a class, discuss, and proceed in the unit they were studying. (A bookmark may come in handy for students to keep their places in the unit proper.) |
| *Information gap* | The actual activities are printed with the instructions for each group or individual student on different pages, so that the participants will not see each other's instructions. Don't allow students to prepare ahead of time or to "cheat" by looking at each other's instructions – the whole point of the communication activities is to *reveal* information to some students and *withhold* it from others who must try and get it. This creates the "information gap" or "uncertainty" mentioned at the beginning as one of the essential ingredients of genuine communication. |
| *Procedure* | In the communication activities, you have to trust the book to control the conversation; only step in when things are going too slowly or too fast. Try not to interrupt the flow of conversations in any way, but monitor the conversations and give help where it is needed. You may have to stop the activity at some point to make time for the very important discussion period. The students then report on what they did, and you and the class discuss their performance – not as actors but as speakers of English. The remarks made above on the procedures for freer exercises apply equally well to handling communication activities, particularly the remarks on monitoring the conversations, repeating activities, changing partners, and recording. |

| | |
|---|---|
| *Teacher's notes* | The complete "route" through the communication activities for each unit is provided. There is also a brief description of the topic of each activity and a note on each student's or group's role, so that you can see at a glance how the activity works. Wherever necessary, there is a note on how to work with an extra student. |

## Written work

| | |
|---|---|
| *Content* | The written work section at the end of every unit gives more opportunities for experimenting with different ways of expressing the functions dealt with in the unit. It is intended to bring together much of what has been covered in the unit and is a useful check on what has been mastered and where problems still lie. |
| *Procedure* | It is best to discuss each piece of written work with the students before they tackle it and to decide together on some good ways to deal with it. If you assign it as homework, make sure your students know exactly what to do. You may have to spend some time on mistakes when you hand written work back – focus more on how well students have communicated their thoughts than on correct grammar and spelling. |
| *Teacher's notes* | The opening lines of a possible version of each written task are given. Very often this is a good way of showing students how to start confidently – the rest is up to them. These opening lines are just suggestions; they are not intended to be models. |

## Conclusion

*Functions of American English* may be a little different from what you are used to, but since real-life communication is so often unpredictable, a course that aims to teach it must in some ways be unpredictable too. During a lesson it is important to be flexible and to allow things to happen that you haven't planned – as long as they are within the scope of the course. In this way, classroom communication can become even more true to life. We hope that you and your students will enjoy using this course and that you will find it helps you to stimulate each other to communicate.

# 1 *Talking about yourself, starting a conversation, making a date*

*Note*: Make sure that the students have read the *Introduction to the student* in their books to get a brief overview of what they are about to do. (Have them read it section by section and ask you about anything that they do not understand. The *Introduction to the teacher* may help you to answer their questions.)

## Functional objectives

In this unit, the students and the teacher will get to know each other; the teacher will then tailor the course (or the emphasis of lessons) to suit the needs and interests of the class; the students will extend their ability to make contact with strangers, to talk about themselves, to get others to talk about themselves, and to arrange meetings with people.

## Presupposed knowledge

Students should already know:
- the necessary vocabulary to describe their background, education, job, and interests
- how to break the ice by talking about the weather

The exercises in this unit will show the gaps in your class's knowledge. But you may want to ask around the class, making sure each student can name his or her job, hobbies, and educational qualifications before you begin the unit.

## 1.1 *Conversation* 🔳

The setting: a crowded cafeteria-style restaurant. Anne is sitting alone, and John (who does not know Anne) approaches . . .

Begin with Student's Books closed. Play the tape through once for general meaning. Play it again, stopping the tape after each example of one of the functions highlighted in this unit (see title of unit and functional objectives). Ask students to tell you what the speakers said, and write these examples on the board.

Finally, you may want to play the tape again and ask students to underline the examples in their books.

The following is a transcript of the conversation, with the functions focused on in this unit labeled on the left and the expressions used to carry out the functions in *italics*.

| | | |
|---|---|---|
| starting a conversation | John: | *Excuse me, is anybody sitting here?* |
| starting a conversation | Anne: | Uh no . . . no, here, let me move my purse from the chair. |
| | John: | Oh, thank you. *Say, haven't I seen you with* Jack Davidson? |
| | Anne: | I work with Jack Davidson. How do you know Jack? |
| getting someone to talk about herself | John: | Oh, Jack and I went to school together. *What sort of work do you do?* |
| getting someone to talk about himself | Anne: | Oh, I . . . I work on commercial accounts at the trust company with Jack. Um . . . *what do you do?* |
| introducing yourself | John: | I'm a telephone installer – I just happen to be working on this street the last couple of days. *I should introduce myself – my name's John Spencer.* |
| introducing yourself | Anne: | *Well pleased to meet you! I'm* Anne Kennedy. |
| getting someone to talk about herself | John: | Happy to know you. *Do you live around here?* |
| | Anne: | Yeah, I live in the neighborhood – it's real convenient to work. |
| | John: | Oh, it sounds like . . .<br>[*fade*] |
| making a date | John: | *. . . Are you doing anything tonight?* |
| refusing an offer of a date | Anne: | Oh . . . uh, *sorry, I'm afraid I'm busy tonight.* |
| making another date | John: | *Well how about tomorrow? Maybe we could go to a movie.* |
| accepting an offer of a date | Anne: | *Hey, that sounds like a great idea!* Um . . . do you like comedies? |
| | John: | Oh yeah, I like comedies . . . uh, let's see what could we see? How about *Bread and Chocolate*? I think that's playing over at . . . |
| | Anne: | Ah . . . |
| | John: | . . . on Main Street there. |
| | Anne: | That's a great idea. |
| | John: | Well I guess, uh, we should meet about eight o'clock then, 'cause I think the movie starts about eight-thirty. Uh, where would be a good place to meet? |
| | Anne: | There's . . . uh . . . there's a clock tower near the movie theater. We could meet there at about eight. |
| | John: | OK. That sounds good. See you tomorrow, then. |
| | Anne: | I'll see you then. Goodbye! |
| | John: | Bye-bye. |

---

## 1.2    *Presentation: talking about yourself* 🔲

Discuss with the class the sort of questions you would ask someone you have just met. For example:

*Do you live near here?*
*Where do you come from?*
*What do you do?*

Point out that the pair work in the next section will enable them to relax, since they will be talking without an audience, and to concentrate on finding things out rather than expressing themselves with complete accuracy. It also means that they are on their own to some extent – so they should call you over and *ask you* if they are at a loss for words or can't express themselves satisfactorily.

| 1.3 | *Exercise in pairs* |
|---|---|

Sit beside a confident student and demonstrate how you want the class to continue.

*Hello. May I introduce myself? My name's Leo—what's yours? Oh, I haven't heard that name before; how do you spell it? Where do you come from? Do you live downtown or in the suburbs? What kind of house do you live in? And what do you do? . . .*

Be friendly and tell your partner about yourself at the same time.
Before students begin working in pairs, check that they understand what they have to do. (Make one group of three if you have an odd number of students.)

| 1.4 | *Exercise in pairs* |
|---|---|

Put students into different pairs from 1.3 (with one group of three if necessary). Since you will want to read the completed questionnaires afterward at your leisure, it might be a good idea for students to use their own paper rather than write in their books. Go around helping each pair. Discuss the exercise with the class:

*Did you find it easy to fill out?*
*Did you and your partner write down different things?*
*Was there a question you couldn't answer?*
*Was there any extra information you wanted to give?*

Read (and correct) the completed questionnaires. Use the information to tailor your course to your students' needs and interests. If you plan to ignore some students' expectations, explain why you intend to do so.

| 1.5 | *Exercise as a class* |
|---|---|

Everyone stands up and circulates. If any group spends too long together, step in yourself as host or hostess and whisk guests away to another part of the party:

*Now then, A, I want you to meet someone who's been dying to meet you.*
or
*A, come and meet B – I'm sure you two will have a lot in common.*
or
*A, have you met B? He comes from . . .*

Afterward, talk about the activity. If students found it difficult, find out why and offer advice.

(If there is time before you get to the next section in class, ask the students to study it at home.)

## 1.6    *Presentation: starting a conversation*

Use the tape. Play it through once to get the general points across. Then play the tape again, pausing for repetition and discussion of how to use each expression. Alternatively, if the students have prepared the section ahead of time, ask them to give you some opening gambits. Write each one on the blackboard, practice pronunciation, and discuss how to use each expression.

You may wish to review words that describe the weather and expressions commonly used when talking about it (such as *Well, let's hope it lasts; Boy, it's nice out today*). Note that people using these expressions do not really want a detailed discussion about the weather; they just want to open the conversation. Ask for more ideas on how to start a conversation, such as:

*It's a beautiful day, isn't it?*
*Sorry to disturb you, but what's that you're drinking?*
*Excuse me, aren't you Mr. A?*
*Would you like a cigarette?*

To practice these opening gambits, get the class to imagine they are all sitting in the reception area of an office or the lounge of an airport. They should start a conversation with the "stranger" beside them.

## 1.7    *Communication activity in two groups*

Divide the class into halves: group A and group B (perhaps have students wear or carry tags labeled A or B). Students in group A all look at communication activity 151 and students in group B look at communication activity 38. Allow time for reading, and check that everyone knows what they have to do. Then tell everyone to stand up. Group A students have to start conversations with group B students. Don't let the conversations go on for longer than a minute or so. If necessary, shout out "change partners!" at regular intervals. Go around monitoring.

When several conversations have taken place, stop this part of the activity and tell everyone in group A to look at communication activity 136 and everyone in group B to look at activity 16. Allow time for reading. Now group B students have to start conversations with group A students. Go around monitoring again.

After several conversations, stop everyone and discuss the activity with the class by asking what went wrong and what was difficult. Tell the class what you heard while you were monitoring. If necessary, replay part of the activity.

*In brief*:
In the first part, group A looks at activity 151 while group B looks at activity 38.
In the second part, group A looks at activity 136 while group B looks at activity 16.

(If you have an odd number of students, so that group A is larger than group B, you may need to join in yourself as a member of group B.)

## 1.8    *Presentation: making a date*

Ask for alternative ideas and write them on the blackboard:

MAKING A DATE:    *Do you have any plans for Saturday?*
                 *What are you doing over the weekend?*

YES!             *That sounds like a really nice idea, thanks.*
                 *It's very nice of you to ask me, thanks.*

NO!              *I'd love to come, but the problem is . . .*
                 *Sorry, I've got to baby-sit tonight.*
                 *Thanks for the offer, but I'm afraid not.*
                 *It's really nice of you to ask, but . . .*
                 *I'd really like to, but the problem is . . .*

Note that these are *not* just pickup techniques. They are needed for arranging to meet acquaintances and friends. However, most of the expressions (such as *Are you doing anything tonight?*) should only be used in situations where it is quite clear what is being suggested (*I was wondering if you'd like to go to a movie*). Otherwise, such expressions can sound like propositions.

What you may say before: introduce yourselves, talk about the weather, discuss topics of general interest.

What you may say after: arrange time and place of meeting, or suggest another day:

*Fine, let's meet outside . . .*
*OK, where shall we meet?*
*How about tomorrow night, then?*
*Could you make it next week?*
*Would Saturday be convenient?*

## 1.9    *Exercise (pattern conversation)*

This kind of exercise with a short model conversation and a set of cues will be called a "pattern conversation" in this book.
The pattern conversation should begin under your close control. Check on pronunciation, tone of voice, and ease of expression to begin with.
Then encourage students to:
1 use different expressions each time
2 leave the pattern and improvise

When the students seem confident, allow them to work on their own in pairs. At the end, ask each pair to perform one conversation without books in front of the class. Ask for comments.

## 1.10    *Exercise as a class*

An alternative to this is to give each student a slip of paper or "role card" telling him or her what to do. The aim of the game is for each player to get as many acceptances as possible to his or her invitation. Here are some suggestions, but your own topical/local ideas are better for your class.

1   You want to have a really good dinner some evening soon. Find an evening when as many others as possible can come. Write down their names.

2   You want to drive to a park for the day on Saturday. See who else would like to come with you. Everyone has to bring their own food for a picnic. Write down enough names for one carful.

3   You want to go to a health food restaurant for lunch tomorrow. See who else would like to come. Write down their names.

4   You want to go out for a pizza for lunch tomorrow. See who else would like to come. Write down their names.

5   There's a good documentary on TV tonight about your country. Find some other people to watch it with you at your place. You'll provide food and drinks. Write down their names.

6   There's a sentimental, romantic movie playing at a theater downtown. See who wants to go with you tomorrow night. Write down their names.

7   Get some people to go with you tomorrow evening to a new bar that just opened. Write down their names.

8   Find some people who would like to go to a disco with you tonight. Write down their names.

9   Find some people who want to do some cross-country skiing with you this Sunday. Write down their names.

10   There's going to be a good classical concert on Thursday. Find some people to go with you (tickets are half-price for students). Write down their names.

11   Get as many people as possible to go swimming and sunbathing with you over the weekend. Write down their names.

12   There's a James Bond movie on TV this evening but you don't have a TV set. Find someone who's going to watch it and see if you can get an invitation.

13   Get some people to go to a historical site with you over the weekend. Write down their names.

14   See who is interested in playing tennis after school this afternoon. You need three others to play doubles. Write down their names.

15   There's a sexy, violent movie playing in town. See who wants to go with you tonight. Write down their names.

Since this is the last oral exercise in this unit, monitor the activity carefully to assess how well the students are doing. Refer back to the functional objectives – have they been achieved? Does more work need to be done on any aspect?

You may also want to discuss with the class some signals people use when they don't want to talk: turning away, giving a one-word answer, starting to read a magazine, etc. How would the students react to such signals?

*Written work*

These suggested opening lines are *not* intended to be models. They just give an idea of one possible way of approaching each topic:

1   A: Excuse me, do you mind if I sit here?
    B: No, of course not. I'll just move my coat.
    A: Thanks. Nice day, isn't it?
    B: Yeah, it really is.
    A: Would you like a cigarette?
    B: Oh thanks.
    A: You might find them pretty strong.
    B: Oh that's all right. I like strong ones.
        etc.

2   Dear John,
      Since this is my first letter to you, let me start by introducing myself and telling you something about myself. My name is Anna and I was born in Hungary, though I spent most of my childhood in Germany. I left school in . . . and started working for . . .

3   Dear Peter,
      I guess you're a little surprised to hear from me after such a long time. My reason for writing is to say how much I enjoyed your company and to invite you to come and stay with me and my family. I've told them a lot about you and they are really looking forward to meeting you . . .

# 2    *Asking for information: question techniques, answering techniques, getting more information*

## Functional objectives

Students will extend their ability to introduce questions politely, to delay answers or avoid replying, and to get people to give more details.

## Presupposed knowledge

Students should already know how to:
– form yes–no questions (*Did you get what you wanted?*), information (Wh-) questions (*Who did you give it to?*), and embedded (or indirect) questions (*I'd like to know when you'll be finished*)
– ask questions with the appropriate intonation

2.1    *Conversation* 🔲

The setting: Anne meets her friend Sue by chance and stops Sue to ask her a few questions . . .

The following is a transcript of the conversation, with the functions focused on in this unit labeled on the left and the expressions used to carry out the functions in *italics*.

|  |  |
|---|---|
|  | Sue:   Hi, Anne! |
|  | Anne:  Oh hi, Sue! |
| leading up to question<br>delaying an answer | Sue:   Uh listen, *I was wondering if you could help me. Do you happen to know* where there's a good place to buy art supplies? |
|  | Anne:  *I'm not really sure. Hey, let me think for a minute.* Oh yeah, there's that new place, Mixed Media – you know, it's down on Main Street? |
|  | Sue:   Mm, I don't know that store – exactly where on Main Street? |
|  | Anne:  Well, you know where the new vegetarian restaurant is – it's right up a block. |
|  | Sue:   Oh yes, I know where you mean now. |
| leading up to a question | Anne:  Hey, *I hope you don't mind my asking, but* are you taking up painting? |
|  | Sue:   [*laughs*] Are you kidding? I can't paint! I'm just asking for my sister's son. He's really into it. |
|  | Anne:  Ah . . . oh, I see. Hey, are you still doing your photography? You're really good at that. |
|  | Sue:   Yeah, that's the one thing I really enjoy. |
| leading up to a question | Anne:  Hey listen. *This may sound like a dumb question, but* can you get any good pictures on an automatic? |

18

|                              |       |                                                                                                                                                                      |
| ---------------------------- | ----- | -------------------------------------------------------------------------------------------------------------------------------------------------------------------- |
| delaying an<br>answer        | Sue:  | No, no, no, now *that's a very interesting question*. Automatics are OK, except for special effects, or stop-action.                                                  |
| getting more<br>information  | Anne: | Oh, and it . . . listen, *there's something else I was wondering about* – like, should you do all your own developing?                                               |
|                              | Sue:  | Oh no! You don't have to develop your own. You can get good prints if you send them out.                                                                              |
| getting more<br>information  | Anne: | No kidding! *Could you tell me something more about* it – like, if I was going to set up a darkroom, what would I really be using it for – what kind of equipment would I need? |
|                              | Sue:  | Oh well, you'd need your enlarger, and . . . and chemicals, but actually developing is only cheaper when you're doing a lot of enlargements.                          |
| leading up to a<br>question  | Anne: | Oh, I see. *Can I ask if* you're making any money at it?                                                                                                             |
| avoiding an<br>answer        | Sue:  | [*laughs*] Well, I'm making enough, and . . . well, it's tax time, so *that's something I'd rather not talk about.*                                                  |
|                              | Anne: | [*laughs*] I really understand. Well, I got to be getting along now, so, so long!                                                                                    |
|                              | Sue:  | Bye!                                                                                                                                                                  |

Here is an alternative to using this conversation that you can use if there is a student with an unusual background or with knowledge of an unusual subject: Ask him or her questions about it and encourage the class to ask questions too. Point out that very direct questions may sound like a police interrogation – questions often need to be introduced politely.

---

## 2.2    *Presentation: question techniques*

The appropriateness of the opening expressions listed here may depend on whether the information asked for is:
a) simple facts
b) complicated, difficult to define
c) personal, potentially embarrassing

Examples of questions that would *not* be appropriate to ask a stranger:
a) *I hope you don't mind my asking, but I'd like to know what time the Chicago train leaves.*
b) *What condition is your country's economy in?*
c) *Why did you leave your wife?*

---

## 2.3    *Exercise as a class*

| Examples of general information: | Examples of personal information: |
| -------------------------------- | --------------------------------- |
| Population of the United States  | Married?                          |
| How much an airplane ticket to London costs | How many children?     |
| What's playing at the movies     | Where do you live?                |
|                                  | How much do you earn?             |

Correct mistakes in grammar and in appropriateness. Demonstrate some of the *delaying* techniques and *avoiding* techniques to be presented in 2.4. Make a mental note of the questions asked in this exercise as ammunition for exercise 2.5.

## 2.4 *Presentation: answering techniques*

Ask for more ideas on how to delay your answer, such as:

*I'll get back to you later on that.*
*Could I answer that one later? I need to look it up.*

Ask for more ideas on what to say when you don't know the answer:

*I really don't know.*
*I'm sorry, I have no idea.*
*You know, I really can't remember.*

## 2.5 *Exercise as a class*

Ask the members of the class some slightly embarrassing personal questions as well as some difficult questions of fact about, for example, their birthplace.
Correct inappropriate answers. Suggest better ways of answering.

## 2.6 *Communication activity in pairs*

Student A: part one – activity 40      part two – activity 57
Student B: part one – activity 109      part two – activity 124
(If you have an odd number of students, form one group of three with two students working as A.)

In part one, student B finds out from A about the Beatles' career from 1956 to 1964. A has all the facts; B has a sheet with missing information.
In part two, student A finds out from B about the Beatles' career from 1965 to 1970.

Begin by reminding the students that they should only look at their own page, not their partner's. Allow time for preparatory reading and questions first. Perhaps point out that although the information is in note form, students' questions should be complete sentences, and answers should be appropriate.

After the activity is over, ask the students to report what difficulties they had in communicating and in phrasing questions. Make your comments on their "performance."

## 2.7 *Presentation: getting more information*

As an example, take a description of someone's job:

A: I work in an office.
B: What do you do exactly?
A: You know, I answer the phone and stuff like that.
B: REQUEST FOR EXTRA INFORMATION

## 2.8     *Exercise in class*

Allow time for preparation. Perhaps get students to work out a few humorous (or even nasty) questions.
Be evasive in answering. Force them to use expressions from 2.7. Correct mistakes.

## 2.9     *Communication activity in groups of four*

Student A:  activity 99
Student B:  activity 92
Student C:  activity 44
Student D:  activity 8 (can be left out)

Each student has some information about a famous inventor:
Student A is an expert on Alexander Graham Bell.
Student B is an expert on Henry Ford.
Student C is an expert on Thomas Alva Edison.
Student D is an expert on the Wright Brothers.

Each biography gives similar information about the person's life and what he is famous for. The idea is for the non-experts to find out as much as possible from the expert.

Allow time for reading and questions before the activity begins. You may need to help some students during the activity. Finish by discussing what each group found out. You may want to include some short exchanges on the impact of the inventions on the world.

## 2.10     *Consolidation exercise in pairs or small groups*

Monitor each group carefully (perhaps record one or more groups).
Report to the class afterward and tell them their strong points in this activity and what skills they still need to improve.
If necessary, rearrange groups and repeat the exercise for improved performance.
Have the functional objectives been achieved?

## 2.11     *Written work*

Possible openings:

1 Dear Sir:
     I saw your ad in the *Post*, and then a colleague of mine, Mr. Johnson, recommended your hotel to me. He is a regular guest of yours.
     Could you please give me the following information . . .

2 Dear Michael,
     It must be more than three years since we spent an evening together. I really must apologize for not keeping in touch.
     Well, a lot of things have happened here. For a start, I'm not only married, but I have a little daughter. Yes, I finally married Mary and . . .

# 3  Getting people to do things: requesting, attracting attention, agreeing and refusing

## Functional objectives

Students will extend their ability to make requests appropriately, to attract someone's attention, to agree or refuse to do something, and to give a reason or make an excuse.

---

## 3.1    Conversation 🔲

The setting: Bob and Mary Graham go to a new restaurant with a very busy waitress . . .

The following is a transcript of the conversation, with the functions focused on in this unit labeled on the left and the expressions used to carry out the functions in *italics*.

|  |  |  |
|---|---|---|
|  | Bob: | Well, what do think of this, Mary? Do you like this restaurant? |
|  | Mary: | Oh, honey, it looks very nice. Oh, look, let's see if we can sit over there by the window so we can look at the water! |
| attracting attention and requesting | Bob: | Oh yeah, sure. *Uh, hm, excuse me miss, could we* have a table over there by the window? |
| refusing one request, giving a reason, and making another request | Waitress: | Nuh, *I'm sorry, we're closing that section. Would you mind* sitting over here? |
| agreeing to a request | Mary: | Oh . . . oh, *all right, sure.* |
|  | Bob: | Mm . . . Well, OK, I wonder what's on the menu. |
|  | Mary: | I'm starving. |
|  | Bob: | We don't have a menu. There's not one on this table. |
|  | Mary: | Oh. |
| requesting | Bob: | Mary, *d'you think you could,* uh, ask those people over there . . . |
| agreeing to a request; attracting attention, and requesting | Mary: | *Oh sure,* honey. Just a minute. Um, *excuse me, I wonder if we* could . . . oh, I'm sorry . . . honey, they don't have one either. |
| attracting attention and requesting | Bob: | Oh? |
|  | Mary: | Oh, I'll ask the waitress. *Waitress! Um, we'd like a menu please.* |
| agreeing to a request | Waitress: | Oh, I'm sorry. *Yes of course, here you are.* |
|  | Mary: | Thank you. |
| requesting | Bob: | Thanks. Ah, miss, *could you tell me, what's the "soup of the day"?* |

|  | Waitress: | Well, the "soup of the day" is cream of asparagus. |
|---|---|---|
|  | Mary: | Oh. |
| requesting } | Bob: | Ah. Well, *could you tell me* the . . . about your "specials"? |
|  | Waitress: | Oh. Well, the "special" today is spaghetti. |
|  | Bob: | Uh-huh. Well, if you were going to be eating here yourself, what a . . . what would you have? What's really good? |
|  | Waitress: | Mm . . . I'd recommend the steak . . . |
|  | Bob: | Steak. |
|  | Waitress: | . . . we have really good beef here, yeah . . . |
| requesting }<br>agreeing to a }<br>request } | Mary: | OK. *Well, give me* a couple of minutes to think about it, *OK?* |
|  | Waitress: | *OK.* I'll be right back. |
|  | Mary: | OK. |
|  | Bob: | Thanks. |

An alternative to using this conversation is to get members of the class to do things for you, such as open the window, open the door, pick up your pen, clean the board, change places, etc.

---

## 3.2    *Presentation: requesting*  📼

Examples of (a):
opening the window
going downtown to buy something
phoning somebody for you

Examples of (b):

| strangers | boss |
|---|---|
| good friends | school principal |
| colleagues | child |

Good friends can use the least polite forms even when the request may be difficult to fulfill:

*Hey, I need your car.*
*You don't have twenty bucks, do you?*

Ask for other ways to make requests:

| ★ | *I want you to . . .* |
|---|---|
| ★ | *You wanna . . . ?* |
| ★★ | *Can you . . . ?* |
| ★★★★ | *Would you please . . . ?* |
| ★★★★★ | *I'm sorry to bother you, but is there any chance of your . . . -ing for me, please?* |

Note that adding a *please* has the effect of adding a "politeness star."
Note also that an inappropriate tone of voice can remove several stars. Too polite an expression can sound sarcastic (very rude):

*I wonder if you could possibly manage to arrive earlier next time?*

## 3.3 Exercise as a class

A bag or box of props is helpful in this exercise. You can then actually give students the things they ask for. The props include:

pens, paper, eraser, scissors, etc.
coins and real or play money
books, newspapers, magazines
mirror, comb, nail file, etc.

Correct inappropriate requests (or pretend to be offended by rudeness). Agree to do things requested appropriately.

## 3.4 Communication activity in pairs around the class

Student A: part one – activity 80    part two – activity 110
Student B: part one – activity 47    part two – activity 25
(If you have an odd number of students, the extra one can team with an A or a B.)

Allow time for thinking; then in part one all student As go around the classroom asking each student B to do something different for them. In part two, the student Bs do the asking.

Monitor what goes on, paying particular attention to appropriateness. Afterward report to the class on what they did well and what needs improvement. Play again if necessary.

## 3.5 Exercise as a class

Play each of the different roles for a few minutes. Make it crystal clear which role you're playing – react to requests in character with the role you are playing. Step out of your role to correct inappropriate requests.

## 3.6 Communication activity in pairs around the class

Student A: part one – activity 41    part two – activity 123
Student B: part one – activity 61    part two – activity 86
(If you have an odd number of students, the extra one can team with an A or a B.)

In part one, all student As have a list of requests, and all student Bs have to select a role and make a badge or label to identify themselves to others. Make sure there are several different roles in group B. In part two, the situations are reversed. All students should stand up during this activity.

Monitor for appropriateness. If necessary, stop everyone and make them start again. Discuss their success at the end.

## 3.7    *Presentation: attracting attention, agreeing and refusing* 🔲

Ask for other ideas on how to do the following:

attract someone's attention
*Um . . .*
*[Cough]*
*Oh, John, . . .*

agree
*By all means.* ~~Sure~~
*Yes, all right.* ~~I'll be happy to do . . .~~
*Well, OK, I suppose so.* ~~I'd rather not, but~~
*Certainly.*

refuse
*Certainly not!* (Rude)     ~~I'm sorry. I don't have time~~
*I'd rather not if you don't mind.*
*I certainly will not!!* (Rude)
*I'm not up to . . .*

Discuss possible *excuses* for not wanting to lend money:
*Sorry, I'm broke myself.*
*I don't have any change on me.*
etc.

## 3.8    *Exercise (pattern conversation)* 🔲

Check tone of voice first as students perform in front of the class. When ready, encourage them to work on their own in pairs using a variety of expressions and excuses, and then later encourage them to leave the pattern completely and improvise. After that, ask for a public performance of one conversation from each pair of students.

## 3.9    *Communication activity in pairs around the class*

Student A: part one – activity 53     part two – activity 150
Student B: part one – activity 1     part two – activity 108
(If you have an odd number of students, the extra one can team with an A or a B.)

In part one, all student As have a list of requests that they have to get a student B (a "stranger") to agree to before they can move on. The student Bs (who remain seated) have a list of possible excuses, but they have to decide whether to agree or refuse each request. Part two reverses the situation.

Monitor what goes on and report to the class on what they did well and what needs improvement.

## 3.10    *Communication activity in groups of two or three*

There are three separate situations, each of which requires one student to ask for help while the other two are in a position to agree (or refuse) to help.

Part one:    *Hotel robbery at 6 a.m.*
Student A: activity 93, Students B and C: activity 17

Part two:    *Assigning the day's work in an office*
Student B: activity 71, students A and C: activity 100

Part three: *Organizing a big picnic*
Student C (or A in group of two): activity 132, students B and A: activity 2

After finishing each part, discuss or describe one version of the situation as a class before moving on to the next part.

Monitor the activity (and perhaps record one or two groups) and report to the class on the quality of their English performance.
Have the functional objectives been achieved?

## 3.11    *Written work*

Some possible beginnings:

1 Dear Uncle Alan,
   I am writing to you to say how much I enjoyed the week I spent at your summer home on Cape Cod. I really had a very enjoyable time there. Since then my luck has changed and the worst thing is the car accident I was in. I think my father told you about it . . .

2 Dear Johnny,
   I am sorry to have to tell you that I can't lend you the $5,000 you asked for. I can see, of course, that the accident was only partly your fault, but there's no excuse for not insuring the car properly. It's time you found out that . . .

3 A: Excuse me!
   B: Yes, what's the matter? Why are you knocking on the door at this time of the morning?
   A: I'm sorry, but you see I've just been robbed.
   B: Robbed! How did it happen?
   A: I was just taking a bath and . . .

# 4 Talking about past events: remembering, describing experiences, imagining What if ...

## Functional objectives

Students will extend their ability to help other people to remember their past activities and talk about them, to talk about their own experiences, and to imagine what might have happened otherwise.
(Note that unit 14: *Telling a story* continues the theme of this unit.)

## Presupposed knowledge

Students should already know:
- common irregular verb forms
- how to make questions and statements using the simple past (*I showed him ...* ), the past continuous (*I was working there when ...* ), the present perfect (*I've worked there since ...* ), and the past perfect (*I'd retired by the time they ...* )
- how to use the past unreal conditional to make hypothetical statements about the past (*That would never have happened if I had been there*)

---

**4.1** | *Conversation*

The setting: Bob and his friend John are in a bar. Bob remembers the time he almost got married, before he ever met his wife Mary ...

Alternatively, tell the class about one of your own experiences, encouraging them to ask you questions. You could record this as it happens or get someone to interview you on tape before the lesson.

---

**4.2** | *Presentation: remembering*

You can practice these types of questions by getting the class to imagine what they would ask the storyteller in 4.1 (or you if you told them about one of your experiences). Demonstrate the use of *As far as I remember ...* in answers.

---

**4.3** | *Exercise as a class*

Correct mistakes and encourage a variety of expressions.

## 4.4      *Communication activity in pairs*

Student A: activity 22
Student B: activity 79
(With an odd number of students, the extra one works as a team with A.)

Each student has a diary page that outlines what happened to him or her on Friday, March 13. First A has to find out what B did that day; then B has to find out what A did. There may be some argument toward the end! Point out that A and B are "acquaintances," not good friends.
Discuss the activity afterward.

## 4.5      *Exercise in small groups*

Perhaps demonstrate by getting one group to find out about *your* last vacation, while the others listen in.

## 4.6      *Presentation: describing experiences*

Demonstrate the use of the questions by asking the class about:

exams they have taken
countries they have visited
competitions they have entered
crimes or accidents or disasters

Note that *Have you ever . . . ?* is often answered with *past* forms:
*Yes, I have. I* went *there in 1974 and I . . .*

Ask for other ideas for beginning the description of an experience:

*It seems like only yesterday . . .*
*It's so long ago I can hardly remember . . .*

## 4.7      *Exercise in groups of three or four*

Monitor each group and report to the class what went right and wrong. Ask each group to report what they found out.

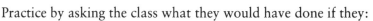

## 4.8      *Presentation: imagining* What if . . .

Practice by asking the class what they would have done if they:

hadn't come to school
had had an accident on the way here
had found some money on the road
had found the school locked today

To practice the negative form of the past untrue conditional, try the following drill. A story based on the illustration in the Student's Book develops while doing this drill. Prepare the class by describing the background to the story:

I went mountain climbing once and I saw a beautiful flower up on a cliff. I decided to climb closer to it, but then ...

Tell the students that to find out the rest of the story, they have to do the following drill using the cues below.

Teacher:      (cue 1) I stepped on a loose rock.
Student A:   (negative question) What would have happened if you hadn't stepped on a loose rock?
Teacher:      (negative of cue 2) I wouldn't have lost my balance.

Teacher:      (cue 2) I lost my balance.
Student B:   (negative question) What would have happened if you hadn't lost your balance?
Teacher:      (negative of cue 3) I wouldn't have slipped.

and so on.

Cues:
1   I stepped on a loose rock.
2   I lost my balance.
3   I slipped.
4   I fell twenty feet.
5   I broke my leg.
6   I was taken to the hospital.
7   I missed my flight home.
8   I met a really nice guy/girl.
9   I got married.
10  We lived happily ever after.

---

## 4.9        Exercise as a class

Ask the class to suggest several different places in the world with different cultures, standards of living, climates, etc.
Correct mistakes and encourage the class to use their imagination. Perhaps have the students prepare in small groups first, with each group concentrating on a different country.

---

## 4.10       Exercise in groups of three or four

Perhaps ask the class to suggest some more events or discoveries that have changed the course of history or the way we live. Encourage them to work out the chain of events that might have occurred, rather than simply how life would be different today. Ask each group to report to the rest of the class.

---

## 4.11       Consolidation exercise in small groups

Monitor each group and report to the class how well they have mastered the expressions introduced in this unit.
Have the functional objectives been achieved?

## 4.12　*Written work*

Some suggested first lines:

1　Dear John,
　　I just have to tell you about a fantastic trip I went on last Saturday. I met Alan and Nora at the bus station and we took a bus to Williamsburg. The trip was really nice – we saw a lot of beautiful scenery and . . .

2　(Pictures are, left to right, Jane Fonda, Muhammed Ali, Paul Newman, Sophia Loren.)
　　If I'd been introduced to Paul Newman, I would have asked him a lot of questions – first of all, I'd have asked him what it's like to be really famous – so everyone recognizes you on the street. I'd have invited him to . . .

3　I'll never forget the day I took my driving test for the first time. I was really nervous about it – my hands were shaking. The first thing the examiner asked me to do was to pull out of the parking lot. I was so nervous I almost forgot to stop at the curb. Then . . .

# 5 Conversation techniques: hesitating, preventing interruptions and interrupting politely, bringing in other people

## Functional objectives

Students will extend their ability to use a variety of hesitation devices, to make sure they are allowed to continue speaking, to interrupt politely, and to encourage other speakers to take part in a discussion. (These techniques lead on to unit 8: *Giving opinions, agreeing and disagreeing, discussing.*)

## 5.1 Conversation

The setting: Sue, John, and Bob and Mary Graham talk about urban development. Sue has some strong opinions ...

Alternatively, start speaking on a topical subject yourself and hesitate a lot. Perhaps record your speech and play it back for analysis. Or record any discussion between native speakers. Note that an impromptu informal conversation is likely to be more hesitant than a prepared formal discussion, where the speakers have rehearsed their points in previous discussions.

## 5.2 Presentation: hesitating

Note that some hesitation devices are occasionally used with their literal meaning:

*He's not an American;* in fact *he comes from Canada.*
*It's over there,* you see?

Ask for other ways to hesitate, such as:

*like*
*as a matter of fact*
*kind of*
*the-the-the* (repetition)
*in-in-in* (repetition)
*I* lengthened to *ay-y*
*to* lengthened to *to-o*
*sort of* lengthened to *sorta-a*

Note that hesitating is a necessary part of taking part in conversations, which are normally unrehearsed and unpredictable: Hesitation gives you time to arrange your thoughts and to choose your words.

## 5.3    Exercise as a class

Alternatively, write these subjects and others on cards and get each student to pick a card at random and then immediately start speaking. The game "Just a Minute" requires speakers to talk for one minute without:

1  stopping
2  repeating
3  deviating from the subject
4  hesitating (but ignore this rule for this exercise)

Further subjects for the cards might be:

| | |
|---|---|
| the police | language labs |
| dinner | cats |
| soup | tea |
| soap | coffee |
| gas | hair |
| expressways | windows |
| why I like this country | pop music |
| why I hate this country | |

Correct mistakes and encourage students to use a variety of hesitation devices.

## 5.4    Presentation: preventing interruptions and interrupting politely 📼

Demonstrate yourself, first by using the "you can't interrupt" techniques and challenging the class to interrupt. Then get a group of students to start talking and try to interrupt them yourself.

Ask for other ideas on interrupting:

*I hate to butt in, but ...*
*There's just one more point I'd like to make ...*

## 5.5    Communication activity in groups of three or four

| | |
|---|---|
| Student A: part one – activity 50 | part two – activity 98 |
| Student B: part one – activity 20 | part two – activity 133 |
| Student C: part one – activity 74 | part two – activity 10 |
| Student D: part one – activity 107 | part two – activity 39 |
| (Student D can be omitted.) | |

In each part, each student is looking at a different aspect of the same general area. They are given a point of view that they have to justify to the others and make them listen:

Part one: smokers' rights

A:  No smoking in public places.
B:  No interference in personal freedom.
C:  Smoking should be illegal.
D:  There should be a higher tax on cigarettes.

Discuss the class's performance in part one before going on to:

Part two: work

A: Workers need longer vacations.
B: Workers don't work hard enough.
C: Machines should do routine jobs.
D: Automation means unemployment.

Again, discuss the activity afterward and report on your monitoring. You may also decide to have the students change roles and discuss the subjects from other points of view.

## 5.6 *Presentation: bringing in other people*

Demonstrate by starting a conversation with one student, then bringing in another student, then another until the conversation snowballs to include everyone.

## 5.7 *Exercise in groups of four or five*

Monitor each group and check that the reticent students are brought into the first discussion. Report to the class and offer advice before they start the second discussion.

## 5.8 *Communication activity in three groups*

Group A: activity 35
Group B: activity 75
Group C: activity 101

Each group or "committee" has to prepare a report to the rest of the class on

A: Their main difficulties with English vocabulary
B: Their main difficulties with English grammar
C: Their main difficulties with English pronunciation

Listen carefully to each report – it may be enlightening. Ask the groups to comment on each other's reports.
Have the functional objectives been achieved?

## 5.9 *Written work*

1  A: Hello, John.
   B:
   A: Fine thanks. What kind of day did you have yesterday?
   B:
   A: Really? I don't believe it.
   B:
   A: All right. I'll take your word for it. What really happened?
   B:

2  A:
   B:  Hello Alan, how are you?
   A:
   B:  Great! You know that car I was thinking of buying – well, I bought
       it!
   A:
   B:  It's true, it's true. And, you know, it was a really good buy.
   A:
   B:  Well, in fact . . .

3  Dear John,
      I'm really sorry I couldn't make our date yesterday. You see, the
   thing is that I met my old teacher. You know, Mr. Jones. And we sort of
   began talking and before I realized it, I missed my bus . . .

# 6 *Talking about the future: stating intentions, discussing probability, considering* What if . . .

## Functional objectives

Students will extend their ability to say how firmly they intend to do something, to say how likely it is for events to happen, and to consider what might happen if the future were different from what is expected.

## Presupposed knowledge

Students should already know how to
- use *will*, *going to*, *may*, *might*, and *could* to refer to future time
- use the simple present to refer to the future (*I leave at noon tomorrow*) and in time clauses (I'll go out *when the weather improves*)
- make hypothetical statements using *if* (*If it rains we'll stay in* or *I would buy it if I had the money*)

---

6.1 | ## *Conversation* 📼

The setting: Anne meets her friend Bob by chance and asks him about his vacation plans . . .

Alternatively, tell the class about your own vacation plans and ask them about theirs. Emphasize the degrees of confidence you have in various plans (see 6.2 and 6.7).

---

6.2 | ## *Presentation: stating intentions* 📼

Demonstrate the use of the expressions by talking about your own plans for the evening – both what you intend to do and what you don't intend to do. Then ask the class to talk about their plans.

---

6.3 | ## *Exercise as a class*

Give the class time to check the lists and mark them.
Then ask each student to speak about his or her intentions. For variety, it might be nice to ask them *Why?* sometimes.

## 6.4     *Exercise in small groups*

Perhaps first ask each student to sketch a map of his or her country/state and put in the names of the neighboring countries/states. This will help them to concentrate.

(If most of your students don't travel much, ask them to talk about different parts of their own country/state.)

## 6.5     *Communication activity in three groups*

Group A: activity 31
Group B: activity 3
Group C: activity 143

Each group is asked to plan a trip and decide what they are going to take. If a group disagrees about the necessity of an item, then it's something they will *perhaps* or *probably* take or not take. If they all agree, then they'll *definitely* take it or not take it. Each group reports to the whole class at the end.

Group A is going by car from Anchorage (Alaska) to Mexico City.
Group B is going to sail around the world on a yacht.
Group C is going to hike along the Appalachian Trail.

Monitor each group and offer advice on needed vocabulary.

## 6.6     *Exercise in small groups*

Monitor each group and throw in ideas to keep the conversations going. Encourage students to use a variety of recommended expressions. Interrupt and ask them to start again, if necessary.

## 6.7     *Presentation: probability*

Demonstrate each expression by talking about tomorrow's weather or next month's weather.

Note that a "tentative" tone of voice shows a lack of certainty, compared with a "confident" tone of voice, when we talk about events that will perhaps happen. Note also that overconfidence is often seen as pomposity or even bluffing.

It's also important to make sure that the students use the correct short answers to the question *Do you think it'll . . . ?*:

√    *Of course it will.*
    *It's sure to.*
    *It's bound to.*

√?    *Probably.*
    *I wouldn't be surprised if it did.*
    *Yes, I think so.*

?? *There's a chance it will.*
*Oh, it might.*
*I guess it might.*

×? *I doubt it.*
*No, I don't think so.*
*There's not much chance.*

× *Of course not.*
*There's no chance.*
*I'm absolutely sure it won't.*

---

## 6.8 *Exercise in small groups*

Madame Zoë knows what will happen in the future. Demonstrate how each group should deal with her predictions:

*She says that ... but I don't think there's much chance of it happening then. Of course it'll happen sometime this century – in fact I wouldn't be surprised if it happened ... years from now ...*

Ask for a report from each group.

---

## 6.9 *Exercise in three groups*

Perhaps look at the items together as a class and agree on the average price of the items today. Add some other items of general interest to the list. Then ask each group to look into their economic crystal balls and predict the prices in five years' time.
Then shuffle the groups so that each new group has former members of each of the first groups – they should argue about or discuss their original estimates.

---

## 6.10 *Exercise in groups*

Perhaps start the ball rolling by talking as a class about changes that have taken place in the past fifteen years. Talk briefly about politics, science and technology, economic affairs, and everyday life.
Ask each group to decide on their predictions before they report to the whole class.

---

## 6.11 *Presentation: considering* What if . . . 

Deomonstrate by saying what you would do/how you would feel/what it would be like if *you* became a millionaire. Then ask the class to make their own suggestions.
Point out the difference between:

*extremely unlikely* future events (using type 2 conditionals
    such as *If he hurried, he would catch the bus*)
*possible* future events (using type 1 conditionals such as
    *If he hurries, he will catch the bus*)

If necessary, practice discussing *possible* future events and their consequences by asking the class to invent sentences from these cues:

nice summer
bad winter
further inflation
election results
TV program
enough time
enough money

For example:

A: *If we have a nice summer this year, how will you feel?*
B: *Oh, I'll be really pleased.*

Note that a useful "rule of thumb" to spot a *possible* future event is the use of:

*It all depends on ...*
as in:
*It all depends on the weather. If it's nice, we'll go out. If it rains, we'll stay in.*

---

## 6.12 Exercise (pattern conversation)

Perhaps remind the class that all the events in the cues are either impossible or extremely unlikely.
Correct mistakes of pronunciation and grammar. Encourage students to use a variety of expressions and then to leave the pattern and improvise.

---

## 6.13 Exercise in small groups

Monitor and encourage each group. Ask them what they would miss most.

At the report stage, perhaps use the "desert island" idea: What would you like to have with you if you were stranded on a desert island? Ask the students what records, books, food, clothes, luxuries, and also what other person they would want to have with them.

---

## 6.14 Communication activity in small groups

1 First, each group has to decide on their plans for the next few days *and* their long-term ambitions.
2 Then, and not until then, allow them to look at activity 9. (This tells them to speculate how their short-term plans would change if they were cut off by snowdrifts.)
3 Then allow them to look at activity 58 (which introduces the unlikely possibility that they never need to work again).
4 Discuss the whole exercise with the class.

*Written work*

Sample openings:

1 Dear Mary,
   You told me about your own vacation plans over the phone the other day. Now I've been thinking and trying to decide what to do myself. I haven't made up my mind yet about going to Europe. If I do, I may go on a package tour to England again . . .

2 *The world in 2100*
   I'll try to make this prediction seem as realistic as possible – but looking this far ahead is really just like science fiction. To begin with, there is likely to be some sort of world government by then, probably not a democracy but a military dictatorship. Life is sure to be much less free than it is now, for example . . .

3 If I were President, the first thing I'd do would be to abolish the armed forces. I'd keep a strong police force to maintain internal security and prevent the Opposition from taking over. In fact I'd probably deport all the Opposition to another country, so that all the people in my country supported me. The next thing I'd do would be to . . .

# 7 Offering to do something, asking for permission, giving reasons

## Functional objectives

Students will extend their ability to offer to do things themselves for other people, to get others to allow them to do something, to give or refuse permission, and to explain why they want to do something.

## Presupposed knowledge

Students should already know how to:
– make requests appropriately (as practiced in unit 3: *Getting people to do things*)
– explain causes and effects (*He dropped the ball, so they lost the game*)
– make excuses (*Sorry I did it, but it was an accident*)

## 7.1 Conversation

The setting: Anne and her new friend John are in the dining area of Anne's apartment. They have just finished dinner . . .

Alternatively, go around the class offering to do things for individual students, like opening windows, lending pens, books, etc., looking at written work. And ask for their permission to do various things, like leaving the room, sitting down, skipping the next lesson. Give your reasons for each.

## 7.2 Presentation: offering to do something

Ask for other ways of offering to do something:

*I'll get it for you.*
*Here, let me help you.*

and accepting an offer:

*Yes, please.*
*Thanks very much.*

and refusing an offer:

*No, it's OK; don't worry about it.*

Practice by telling the class you need various things: pen, paper, book, cassette recorder, paper clip, dictionary, pen or chalk, drink, etc.
Get them to offer to lend, get, or give you what you need. Refuse or accept each offer.

## 7.3 Exercise as a class

Tell the class your problems – the exercise is more productive if you really act the part! Get them to make *offers of help* – not suggestions of what you should do but ways they can help. Correct mistakes.
Continue in pairs if more practice is needed and perhaps ask each pair to perform while the rest of the class listens. Ask for comments.

## 7.4 Communication activity in pairs

Student A: activity 91
Student B: activity 63
(An extra student can share student A's problems.)

Student A begins by telling B each of the problems in his or her list and waiting for an offer of help. Then A hears about B's problems.

## 7.5 Presentation: asking for permission

Examples of (a): opening window if the room is cold *or* stuffy, borrowing a pen *or* a car, leaving five minutes early *or* thirty minutes early.
Examples of (b): boss, teacher, colleague, best friend.

Decide with the class which expression would be appropriate for each combination of the examples.

Ask for other ideas for giving permission:

*Yes, of course you can – go ahead!*
*By all means.*

and refusing permission:

*No, you can't do that!* (very rude)
*I'm afraid that's not really possible.*
*Well, if you did that* . . . followed by description of unpleasant
  consequence

## 7.6 Exercise as a class

Allow each student time to make a list of five things.
The students then ask you for permission and, if relevant, you ask them why they want to do these things.
Then leave the room and come back in the role of head of the school, perhaps wearing a different coat.
Correct mistakes by stepping out of the role.

## 7.7 Presentation: giving reasons 🔲

Decide with the students how they might explain their reasons for wanting to borrow your: pen, watch, shoes, book, jacket, comb, keys, etc.

## 7.8 Exercise (pattern conversation) 🔲

Correct mistakes and offer advice.

## 7.9 Communication activity in pairs

Student A: part one – activity 11    part two – activity 84
Student B: part one – activity 56    part two – activity 114
(An extra student can share student B's part.)

In part one, student B plays in quick succession the roles of boss, friend, and teacher while student A has to ask each "character" for permission to do various things. Both A and B must do the conversations in the order given in the instructions.
In part two, the roles are reversed. Again, the given sequence must be followed.

Monitor for appropriate language and report to the class afterward.

## 7.10 Communication activity in groups of three

Student A: activity 105
Student B: activity 73
Student C: activity 19
(With one or two extra students, one can join B and another C.)

Each "friend" wants to do certain things to help A, who also wants to do certain things. Make sure each student makes his or her own list *before* the groups meet. Perhaps circulate making suggestions.

Monitor each group and report to the class afterward.

## 7.11 Written work

Possible ways to begin:

1 Dear Mary,

   Congratulations on your new job in Brussels! I know you don't have much time before you leave, so maybe I could help you. When you move out of your apartment, would you like me to help you pack your books? If you like I could store them in my attic. Maybe I could also help you . . .

2 Dear Sir:

   I am writing to you on behalf of my English class at Peterson Community College. We would like to hold a barbecue in Indian River Park and I was told that we need your permission. The date we have in mind is . . .

3 Dear Rob,
    I wonder if you remember the last time we met and talked about your cabin on Round Lake. You offered to let me use it for a weekend and I've really been looking forward to taking you up on your offer.
    I wonder if it would be possible for me to go to the cabin with some friends on . . .

# *8* Giving opinions, agreeing and disagreeing, discussing

## Functional objectives

Students will extend their ability to introduce their opinions, to agree or disagree with other people's opinions, to express tentative opinions, and to ask other people to explain their points of view.

## Presupposed knowledge

Students should already know how to:
– use the conversation techniques practiced in unit 5

---

**8.1**  *Conversation* 🔲

The setting: Sue and her friends Ken and Mary discuss violence on TV. Sue has some strong opinions . . .

Alternatively, begin discussing a topic in today's news (perhaps after playing a tape of today's radio news). Introduce your own opinions and ask the class to say what they think.

---

**8.2**  *Presentation: giving opinions* 🔲

Ask for other ideas:

*As far as I'm concerned . . .*
*It seems clear to me that . . .*
*Well, obviously . . .*
*I can't help thinking that . . .*
*What's really happening is that . . .*

Note that the more informal expressions are appropriate for friendly relationships, and the more formal ones for talking to strangers and people older than or senior to yourself.

---

**8.3**  *Exercise (pattern conversation)* 🔲

Perhaps run through this exercise twice: once with A and B as friends, then again with A and B as strangers.

## 8.4 Exercise in groups of three

Monitor each group and offer advice. Get each group to join with another group at the end and exchange opinions.

## 8.5 Presentation: agreeing and disagreeing

Ask for more ideas on how to agree, such as:

*Right!*
*That's absolutely true!*
*I couldn't have put it better myself!*
*I sure agree with that!*

Ask for other ideas on how to disagree, such as:

*That's more or less true, but ...*
*I guess that's partly true, but ...*
*I see what you mean, but ...*
*Yes, but isn't it also true that ...*
*I guess you could say that, but ...*

Note the danger of disagreeing directly except with close friends. Strangers and acquaintances are likely to be quite upset if you say:

*No, you're wrong!*
*I don't agree at all!*
*That's just dumb!*
*No way!*

## 8.6 Exercise (pattern conversation)

Perhaps run through the conversations twice – once with A and B as strangers, then again as friends. Or change the relationship halfway through the topics of conversation.

## 8.7 Communication activity in groups of three

Student A: activity 70
Student B: activity 30
Student C: activity 7
(An extra student or two can share A, B, or C's part.)

Each student is given two strongly held opinions, which the others listen to and react to appropriately. Each group must follow the sequence of instructions in the activities.

## 8.8      *Presentation: discussing* 🔲

To practice these expressions, take a topic from today's news (perhaps record the radio news and listen to it first).
Point out that we sometimes present both sides of an argument using expressions like:

*On the one hand ... ; on the other hand ...*
*It's true that ... ; but it's also true that ...*

## 8.9      *Communication activity in pairs*

Student A: activity 142
Student B: activity 102
(An extra student can team up with A or B – in fact A could be a team of two and B a team of two, making groups of four.)

Each student needs time to prepare his or her ideas before the discussion begins. Then A introduces the topic of *Exams* and puts the case for and against while B listens and reacts. Then B introduces the topic of *Marriage*. Point out that students should give their *own* views on the topics.

Monitor and report on the class's performance.

## 8.10      *Exercise in large groups*

A large class can be divided into several groups; a small class (less than eight) could work as one group. Each group can select a different topic.

The *notes* required are in preparation for 8.12: Written work (2).
These notes might take the form of:

1 Points made that everyone agreed with
2 Points made that there was disagreement about (listing both sides' opinions)
3 Examples given
4 Conclusion of the discussion

## 8.11      *Consolidation exercise: debate as a class*

Decide with the class on a topic that everyone is interested in. It may be best for speakers to prepare their speeches in advance at home. Or small groups can prepare speeches in class before the debate begins. Select a chairperson (ideally a reliable student rather than you; you will need to monitor the speakers). Appoint opening speakers for each side.
Try to find a topic of current interest, but here is one suggested topic:
"The punishment should fit the crime." (Perhaps outline the implications of such a viewpoint on crimes like murder, terrorism, and mugging. And describe the traditional notion of "an eye for an eye, a tooth for a tooth.")

## *Written work*

Suggestions:

1 To whom it may concern:
   Juan Fernandez has been a student of mine since 1977. For as long as I have known him, I have been impressed by his hard work and intelligence. He has been a valuable member of his class: he helps his classmates unselfishly and participates actively in lessons. His written work has improved greatly and is now . . .

2 The discussion began with general agreement that governments need to cooperate on the pollution problem. It was noted that many countries pollute international waters, the air, and rivers that are shared with other countries. Lake Erie was taken as an example. Carl stated that it is already dead but Richard disagreed and said that if action is taken quickly, the lake could be saved . . .

3 We have spent a lot of time discussing the topic of . . . I would like to put my thoughts about it on paper. First of all, I believe that . . . if only because . . . Second, it must be emphasized that . . . and that . . .

# 9 Describing things, instructing people how to do things, checking understanding

## Functional objectives

Students will extend their ability to describe objects, to give people step-by-step instructions on how to do things, to check if the listeners have understood, to give encouragement to someone following their instructions, and also to interrupt and ask for more explanation if instructions are not understood.

## 9.1 Conversation 🔲

The setting: Ken asks his friend Sue how to work an unusual-looking tape recorder, and Sue provides detailed instructions . . .

Alternatively, describe your own cassette player to the class (leave it outside, or put it behind you so the class can see it but you can't). Then explain how it works, without touching or pointing to the controls.

(Note that in fact we often point and touch things, and say things like the following while we're showing someone how to do something: *You do this, Then this. Then this. And this happens* . . . This unit, however, practices the language needed for giving instructions more fully!)

## 9.2 Presentation: describing things 🔲

Ask for suggestions from the class on how to describe different objects. A box of props is essential here. It could contain all sorts of objects: rubber stamp, old alarm clock, gloves, tickets, bottles, pencil sharpener, eraser, etc.

| | |
|---|---|
| Size – general impression: | *tiny, enormous, minute* . . . |
| height, width, depth, length, etc.: | $5'' \times 10'' \times 15''$ (read as "*5 inches high by 10 inches wide by 15 inches deep*" |
| Shape: | *square, circular, rectangular, oval* . . . |
| Color: | *greenish, bluish, sort of brownish red, sort of reddish brown, crimson, navy blue, royal blue* . . . |
| What it's made of: | *plastic, aluminum, stainless steel, leather* . . . |
| What it looks like: | *It looks a little bit like a tube, like a box, like a transparent envelope* . . . |

| What it's used for: | *for attaching papers together, for telling the time, to keep sunlight out of a room ...* |
|---|---|
| How it works: | *You turn the knob on the back to set it and you press the button on the top to turn it off ...* |

With the class, look at each of the objects in your box and around you in the classroom. Write on the board the useful new words they need to describe each one. Allow the class time to make notes.
You can use the following game to practice this:
Fill a bag with some mystery objects. Ask each student to *feel* inside the bag and describe what he or she is touching. The others have to listen and guess what each object is.

---

## 9.3   *Exercise as a class*

Alternatively, try this game:
Write the names of many different objects on cards (or slips of paper) and ask each class member to select a card at random. He or she then has to describe the object without revealing either its name or its use. The idea of the game is to describe the object truthfully but to withhold any information that will give the name of the object away. The others have to listen and guess what each object is.
Here are some objects that could go onto the cards:

| | |
|---|---|
| coat hanger | staples |
| screw | rubber band |
| record | bathtub |
| sunglasses | alarm clock |
| scissors | light bulb |
| armchair | frying pan |
| paper clip | suitcase |

(Add more ideas of your own.)

Correct mistakes and offer suitable vocabulary to help.

---

## 9.4   *Exercise as a class*

Allow some time for silent thinking first. The students should be encouraged to ask about objects they really do want to know the English word for, and about objects they know the word for but think others in the class may not know.
Go around the class asking each student to ask questions.

## 9.5    *Exercise in pairs*

Perhaps suggest an example of each to start them off:

an electric drill
a comb
a sock
a pen
chewing gum

Alternatively, play the following game, which needs a certain amount of preparation but is very useful and quite challenging.

Divide the class into pairs of students, A and B. Student A has a set of twelve cards, and student B has a "plan" that shows how the cards must be arranged and that student A must not be able to see. Goal: Student A must arrange the cards in exactly the same order and the same way up as shown on the plan. The rules are that the plan-holder is not allowed to point and the card-holder is not allowed to ask simply, "Where do I put this one?" In other words, each card must be accurately described by the plan-holder.

After the cards have been correctly laid out, A and B reverse roles: A gets the plan and turns it sideways, being careful not to let B see it. B shuffles the cards and then they play the game again.

After finishing this round, each pair of students can swap cards and plan with the next pair and continue the game.

The "cards" are easily prepared by using two sheets of plain paper with carbon paper in between. Divide the sheets into twelve equal squares using a ruler.

Draw *similar but subtly different* abstract designs on each square:

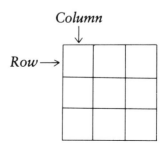

Cut up *one* of the finished sheets and number each card to identify it as part of set 1. Do the same with different designs to complete more sets.

Monitor each pair during the exercise and answer questions. Note that ways of expressing position may need to be reviewed first:

*upside down*
*the other way around*
*in the top left-hand corner*
*at the bottom of the middle column*
*on the right end of the second row*
etc.

*Set of cards*

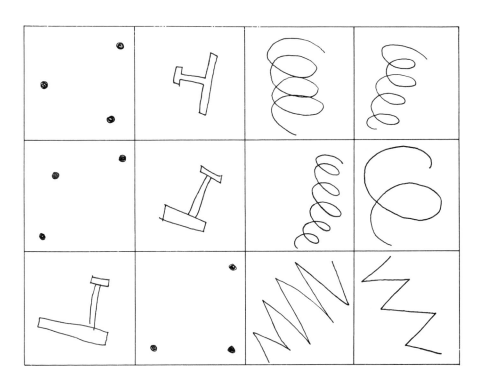

*Plan*

## 9.6     *Presentation: step-by-step instructions*

Point out that written instructions can be much briefer than spoken instructions (because we can re-read sentences several times if we don't understand the first time). Written instructions are often in the form of simple lists. For example:

1 Plug into outlet.
2 Slide cassette into opening under lid.
  NB: Make sure that the tape faces you and that the desired side is up.
3 Check that player is working by doing a trial run: a play–stop–rewind–stop sequence.

Demonstrate by devising a list of instructions for using your classroom tape recorder and then transforming them into spoken instructions.

## 9.7     *Exercise as a class*

Perhaps get the class to begin as pairs to decide together what gadget they are going to explain. Perhaps they could make brief notes to start with. When they are ready, ask each student to explain to you how their gadget works. Before each one starts, identify the role you will be playing:

a less mechanical person than you really are
an old lady
a child
a know-it-all
their boss

Ask the class to comment on how the instructions differ when one is talking to different kinds of people.
Correct the students on inappropriate language.

## 9.8     *Communication activity in pairs*

Student A: activity 52
Student B: activity 104
(An extra student can share A or B's part.)

First of all, A is an expert on *Making tea* and has to tell B the British method. Then B tells A *How to make your own yogurt*.

Monitor the performance of each pair and report afterward. If necessary, ask them to do it again.

## 9.9     *Presentation: checking understanding*

Ask for other ways to check understanding, such as:

*Have you got all that?*
*Are you following me?*
*So far so good?*
*Got it?*

Practice using expressions of encouragement by having the students tell someone how to:

use an electric typewriter or mixer or drill
treat a cut finger or a sprained ankle
take care of someone who has fainted

Perhaps get some more examples of ways for the listener to interrupt long instructions when he or she does not fully understand:

*I didn't catch that last part.*
*I'm not following you.*
*I don't get you.*
*Hold it.*
*Wait a minute.*
*What was that?*
*Come again?*

Demonstrate various ways of checking understanding while giving the class instructions on how to take care of the flu. Get the students to interrupt to ask for clarification – you can include some unusual remedies to provoke interruptions. You might begin like this:

*"If you think you're getting the flu, the first thing you should do is to go home and rest – OK? Then you should go into the kitchen and boil some water ... "*
(interruption) *"Sorry, but I don't see why the first thing you do at home is boil water."*
*"Ah well, that's because you need a hot drink – it helps you to relax. Do you know what I mean? Now the best way to prepare a relaxing drink is to mix a quarter of a cup of brandy with the juice of one lemon, and then add sugar to taste and fill the cup with boiling water ... "*

---

## 9.10     *Communication activity in pairs and then in groups of four*

Group A: activity 51
Group B: activity 82
(An extra student can become a third member of any pair. An extra pair has to be split between two other pairs.)

Students begin working in pairs. They need enough time to write out their instructions for each of the two activities. Later each pair from group A joins a pair from group B, forming a group of four.

Group A is asked to work out instructions on:
how to play your favorite indoor game
how to make a good cup of coffee

Group B is asked to work out instructions on:
how to cook a favorite dish
how to play your favorite outdoor sport

Monitor each group and offer advice and needed vocabulary.

## 9.11    *Consolidation exercise as a class*

Perhaps ask the students to prepare at home their explanations of item
2 "An activity connected with your hobby or job."
Demonstrate item 1 by telling them how to get to your home.

Monitor and report on the students' performance. Ask them to make their
own comments on their performance.

## 9.12    *Written work*

Some possible openings:

1 It's made of steel and it's made of two parts that are almost identical.
   The two parts are joined together with a screw that is kept fairly loose.
   Each of the parts has one round end and one pointed end. The difference between the two round ends is that one is large enough to
   put your thumb into and the other is large enough to put two fingers
   into . . .

2 *Scrambled eggs*
   (1)  You need a non-stick frying pan, a small bowl, a wooden spoon, some
        eggs (2 per person), a little butter, a little milk, pepper, and salt.
   (2)  Break the eggs into the bowl and add a little milk, and salt
        and pepper to taste. Beat lightly.
   (3)  Melt the butter in the frying pan and when it's hot, add the egg
        mixture.
   (4)  Stir the egg mixture constantly as it cooks . . .

3 *Spanish omelet*
   (1)  Prepare some potatoes by peeling them and boiling them until
        they are just cooked. They must still be firm, not soft.
   (2)  Chop the potatoes into small cubes and put them on a warm plate.
        Keep the chopping board and knife.
   (3)  Chop a large onion into small pieces and fry it in a frying pan in butter
        or olive oil until . . .

Here is an extra idea for written work:

4 Write the instructions on how to carry out one of the processes, or op-
   erate one of the machines you described earlier in this unit.

# 10 Talking about similarities, talking about differences, stating preferences

## Functional objectives

Students will extend their ability to describe and discuss similarities and differences, and to explain their preferences.

## Presupposed knowledge

Students should already know how to:
— use common expressions of quantity, such as

| | |
|---|---|
| *dozens of* | *several* |
| *hundreds of* | *a few* |
| *a huge amount* | *a little* |
| *plenty of* | *some more* |
| *enough* | *none at all* |

— use the forms *more ... than, as ... as, many, much, a lot of, lots of*

## 10.1 Conversation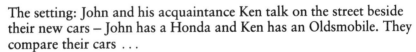

The setting: John and his acquaintance Ken talk on the street beside their new cars – John has a Honda and Ken has an Oldsmobile. They compare their cars ...

Alternatively, prepare a set of magazine ads for different cars – some quite similar, some very different. Talk with the class about these cars, pointing out similarities and differences. These ads can be pinned up in the classroom or for durability glued onto cards, so that they can be held up and passed around.

## 10.2 Presentation: talking about similarities and slight differences

Demonstrate by using the recommended expressions as you state any other similarities that you can think of between the four states – characteristics of the people, education systems, food, etc.

To practice, ask each student to talk about the similarities between the state where he or she lives (or homeland) and one of the four states listed. (Population statistics are for 1970-71.)

## 10.3 *Exercise in small groups*

Monitor each group and correct mistakes. Ask for a report from each group afterward.

## 10.4 *Exercise in pairs or small groups*

A starting point might be to look at ads cut out of a magazine for different cars or other products. Get each group to compare them and report to the class.

## 10.5 *Presentation: talking about differences*

Again, demonstrate by talking about other differences and ask each student to point out differences between his or her state or country and Rhode Island or Texas. (Population statistics are for 1970-71.)

## 10.6 *Exercise in two large groups*

(A very large class may need more groups.)

Make sure that every student in each group gets a turn to talk. Monitor each group and afterward report to the class. (Population statistics are for 1978–80.)

## 10.7 *Exercise in small groups*

Monitor each group and report to the class on their performance.

## 10.8 *Exercise in small groups*

Perhaps ask each group to "specialize" on a different topic, so that the report they make to the rest of the class can be more detailed and interesting.

## 10.9 *Exercise in pairs*

A starting point might be to remind the class what they talked about in unit 1 when they were "Talking about themselves." It might be worth referring back to 1.3.

## 10.10 Presentation: stating preferences

Ask for more ideas on how to state a preference:

*I like ... better because ...*
*For me, the best ...*
*I'd rather do this ...*
*Best thing would be to ...*
*The best one is ...*

To demonstrate and practice, either get a restaurant menu for the class to study and comment on, or with the class's help write a varied menu on the board and ask them to state their preferences.

## 10.11 Exercise in groups of three or four

If possible, add your present city to those in the table by writing information about it on the board. Perhaps include some negative aspects of life in each city, such as crime and slums in New York and Washington, bad public transportation in Houston, earthquakes in San Francisco, and many disappointed gamblers and unhappy divorcees in Las Vegas.
(Population statistics are for metropolitan areas for 1970-71, except New York's figure, which is for 1978-80.)

## 10.12 Consolidation exercise in pairs

It may be necessary to begin by asking the class what they expect from a job – what pay, hours, type of work, etc. If none of the jobs is really appealing, have the students say which is better than the others.
(As additional written work they could "apply in writing" for one of the jobs.)

## 10.13 Written work

Some possible openings:

1 Dear Maria,
  I was delighted to hear that you are going to Scotland next month. Let me tell you some of the things to expect when you get there. To begin with, the weather keeps changing all the time – it seems to rain a lot, but you can never be sure when it's going to rain. Another big difference is that ...

2 *The Sun* and *The Post*
  Both these newspapers are morning papers, and the immediate impression you get is that they are very similar in style and layout. Politically they are both on the right, though neither of them is a party newspaper. As far as their content is concerned, however, ...

3 Discuss this topic with the students before they write anything.

# *11* Making suggestions and giving advice, expressing enthusiasm, persuading

## Functional objectives

Students will extend their ability to give advice to people who aren't sure what to do, to make enthusiastic suggestions, and to persuade people to accept their suggestions.

---

**11.1** *Conversation* 🔲

The setting: Ken visits his friend Sue at her apartment and wants to smoke . . .

Alternatively, tell the class that you are dissatisfied with your "image" – the clothes you wear, your hair and general appearance. Get the students to suggest how you could improve!

---

**11.2** *Presentation: making suggestions and giving advice* 🔲

Ask for other ways to make suggestions:

*How about . . . -ing . . .*
*One idea would be to . . .*
*I'd suggest that you . . .*
*Maybe you ought to . . .*

Get the class to make suggestions to a smoker on how to stop, using each of the expressions.

---

**11.3** *Exercise as a class*

Pretend that you are fed up with your job – ask the students to make suggestions about what you should do. Tell them about your other problems too:

You are lonely.
You find it hard to make friends.
You have dandruff and a bad complexion.
You are out of shape.
You don't know what to do this evening, this weekend,
    and for your next vacation.

Correct mistakes as you go along.

## 11.4 Exercise in small groups

This exercise may have to be changed (or avoided altogether) with students who are refugees. Perhaps begin by asking each student to make a list of his or her friends and relatives back home (possibly inventing some of them).

Monitor each group and report to the class.

## 11.5 Exercise in groups

At the reporting stage, you could ask four students to pretend to be each of the letter writers.

## 11.6 Communication activity in groups of four

Student A: part one – activity 43    part two – activity 144
Student B: part one – activity 33    part two – activity 126
Student C: part one – activity 83    part two – activity 106
Student D: part one – activity 5     part two – activity 64
(Student D can be left out to make one or two groups of three only.)

In part one, each student is given a personal problem, which he or she explains to the others and then asks for advice on. Each problem must be "solved" before the next one is discussed. In part two, there are four more problems.

Monitor each group (perhaps record one or two of the groups in action).

## 11.7 Presentation: expressing enthusiasm

Ask for other ways to express enthusiasm:

*Hey, how about this idea ...*
*I know what we can do – let's ...*
*I'll tell you what – why don't we ...*

Make sure the students use the right tone of voice. Demonstrate and practice by talking about doing something tonight.

## 11.8 Exercise in pairs and as a class

Perhaps start the ball rolling by enthusiastically suggesting:

a dictation next lesson!
a grammar test!!
a review lesson!!!

After preparation in pairs, each pair reports to the rest of the class with enormous enthusiasm.

## 11.9 *Communication activity in groups of three*

Student A: activity 13
Student B: activity 119
Student C: activity 77
(An extra student or two can join A, B, or C.)

Each student has his or her own plans for the weekend, which must be presented enthusiastically to the group. A discussion follows and a compromise plan must be agreed on.

At the end, ask each group to report on their compromise.

## 11.10 *Presentation: persuading*

Ask for other ways to raise objections:

*That's all right in theory, but in practice . . .*
*You don't seem to realize that there's more involved . . .*
*I don't really think that would work because . . .*

and other ways of answering objections:

*Oh yes, but you didn't get the main point . . .*
*You're right, but you've got to realize that . . .*
*Don't let that stop you!*

and perhaps suggest ways of giving in:

*Oh yes, I didn't realize that.*
*Oh no. My idea wouldn't work very well, would it?*
*My god, I hadn't thought of that.*

Practice by telling the class the details of your plan to climb Mt. Everest. Then ask them to suggest their own plan.

## 11.11 *Exercise as a class*

Begin by telling the class how much you smoke, drink, and eat. Ask them to persuade you to cut down or stop. (You know it's all bad for you, but you enjoy smoking, drinking, and overeating.)

## 11.12 *Communication activity in pairs*

Student A: activity 141
Student B: activity 95
(An extra student can join A or B.)

Make sure each pair has time to study their activity pages before they begin talking. A and B have agreed to go on vacation together. A has chosen a hotel in Nassau (Bahamas), B a hotel in Acapulco (Mexico). Each tries to persuade the other.

At the end, ask each pair what decision they reached.

## 11.13    *Communication activity in groups of four*

Student A: activity 72
Student B: activity 29
Student C: activity 4
Student D: activity 117 (can be omitted)

Make sure each student has time to study his or her ad before A begins.
Each student has noticed a different ad: A, a quartz alarm watch; B, a
radio/8-track/record player; C, a radio/thermometer/clock; D, an auto-
matic instant camera. Each has to persuade the others that the purchase
of his or her item is a great idea.

Ask each group to report. Report to them on the monitoring you did.


## 11.14    *Written work*

Some possible openings:

1 Dear Robert,
   I'm very sorry to hear about your difficulty in concentrating on study-
   ing for your exam. I know how important the exam is to you.
   Have you ever thought of staying somewhere else before the exam?
   You could go to a cabin and . . .

2 Dear Richard,
   In answer to your problem, yes, I do have a few ideas. I suppose the
   best thing would be to have a party – not just the usual sort of party,
   but a party with surprises. One thing you could do is . . .

3 Dear Susan,
   I was really very upset to hear about Mike. I'm sure he really will
   come back in a few days. After all, it isn't the first time he's dis-
   appeared, is it? Really, the only thing to do is to . . .

# 12 Complaining, apologizing and forgiving, expressing disappointment

## Functional objectives

Students will extend their ability to point out politely that they are dissatisfied, to apologize for what they have done wrong, to break the news that they have an apology to make, to forgive other people, and to express disappointment.

## 12.1 Conversation 📼

The setting: Mary Graham sees her neighbor Ken and asks if her dog is annoying him. Later, Bob Graham arrives and complains about Ken's new stereo ...

Alternatively, enter the classroom looking upset. Break the news to the class that you have lost their homework, not prepared the lesson, and have to leave early for a dental appointment. Ask them what they would tell your head of department or principal.

## 12.2 Presentation: complaining 📼

Ask for other ways to make a complaint:

*There seems to be something wrong with ...*
*By the way, I've wanted to mention this to you for a while ...*

Point out that a direct complaint beginning with, for example, *Look here!* is dangerous because it will antagonize people, perhaps even start an argument, so that you won't get an apology or replacement of merchandise.

Practice with the class by asking them to imagine (a) what a teacher might do wrong and how they'd complain to a teacher who:

| | |
|---|---|
| ignored some students | didn't give back homework on time |
| had a favorite student | asked too many questions |
| spoke too fast | didn't mark homework in a helpful way |
| arrived late | assigned too much homework |

and (b) how they might express dissatisfaction to a fellow student who frequently:

| | |
|---|---|
| arrives late | chews gum loudly during the class |
| interrupts the class | doesn't listen to what you say to him or her |

Correct mistakes and encourage a variety of suggestions.

## 12.3 Exercise (pattern conversation)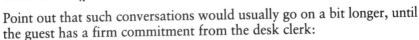

Point out that such conversations would usually go on a bit longer, until the guest has a firm commitment from the desk clerk:

Desk clerk: ... I'll have it looked after right away.
Guest:       How long is it going to take?
Desk clerk: I'll call you in five minutes and let you know.
Guest:       OK.

## 12.4 Communication activity in two groups

Group A:  part one (as storekeepers) – activity 60
                 part two (as customers) – activity 90
Group B:  part one (as customers) – activity 6
                 part two (as storekeepers) – activity 26

In the first part, each student in group A sets up a store (which sells everything) in a different area of the room. Then students from group B go from store to store complaining about the faulty merchandise on their list. In the second part, the roles are reversed.

Monitor each group and make sure each complaint is *politely* expressed.

## 12.5 Communication activity in pairs

Each student follows a rather long route through the communication activities so that each situation is fresh and there is no time for preparation:
Student A goes from activity 128 to 129 to 34 to 23 to 48 to 112
Student B goes from activity 54 to 65 to 116 to 138 to 137 to 89
(With an odd number of students, the extra one can be the husband or wife of A or B.)

First A has a complaint to make to B; then B to A; and so on. It's best if each pair stands up, so that the participants can walk away from each other after each conversation and read what to do next before coming together again.

The complaints are about:

noisy children (neighbors)
nasty dog (neighbors)
blocked driveway (neighbors)
loud TV (neighbors)
stinginess at the bar (friends)
not inviting friend to party (friends)

The complainer must be "satisfied" before he or she goes away.

Monitor for appropriate language. If necessary, interrupt the exercise to make comments.

## 12.6     *Presentation: apologizing and forgiving*

Ask for other ways to apologize:

*There's something I have to tell you.*
*I've got a confession to make.*

and other ways to forgive:

*It's OK. That can happen to the best of us.*
*That's OK – you owe me one!*

Practice by asking the students what they would say to a friend whose dog had run away for two hours while they were supposed to be watching it. Then ask what a hotel receptionist might say to a guest in the following situations:

There is *no* hot water.
Dinner will not be served today.
The room he or she reserved is not available.
He or she has to move to a smaller room.
The air conditioning will be off all day.

Ask the class to suggest more hotel situations from their experience or imagination.

## 12.7     *Exercise (pattern conversation)*

Perhaps do the conversation twice: once with A and B as good friends, then again as acquaintances. Or change roles halfway.
Monitor for appropriate language.

## 12.8     *Communication activity in pairs*

Student A:   part one (as friend) – activity 67
            part two (as friend) – activity 32
            part three (as assistant) – activity 134
            part four (as boss) – activity 120
Student B:   part one (as friend) – activity 36
            part two (as friend) – activity 14
            part three (as boss) – activity 94
            part four (as assistant) – activity 81
(An extra student can share A's roles.)

In each part, both students have an apology to make (for borrowed money not returned, tickets not reserved, car scratched, paint spilled, private call made on office phone, temper lost with assistant, $50 lost, and date canceled unnecessarily).
Monitor for appropriate language. Ask each pair to report to the rest of the class what happened.

## 12.9 Presentation: expressing disappointment

Demonstrate and practice by talking about how the bad weather (storm, snow, rain, hail) has prevented you and your friends from going on the picnic you planned (and the bicycle ride and the trip to the beach).

## 12.10 Exercise (pattern conversation)

Point out and practice the tone of voice usually used to show genuine disappointment and the tone used when taking a disappointment philosophically.
Correct mistakes in grammar and pronunciation.

## 12.11 Communication activity in groups of three

Student A: activity 148
Student B: activity 21
Student C: activity 62
(With one extra student, two students can play C's role together; with two extra students, C can be left out to make a group of two.)

Each student has some bad news to tell his or her friends that he or she knows will disappoint them. They may need to be persuaded to take their setbacks philosophically.

Ask each group to report to the rest of the class on what they did.

## 12.12 Communication activity in pairs

Student A:  part one (as student) – activity 96
             part two (as host or hostess) – activity 145
Student B:  part one (as host or hostess) – activity 87
             part two (as student) – activity 27
(An extra student can share A's role and play "another student" and "host" or "hostess.")

In each part, the "student" has been left alone in the house while the owner of the house is out. The student has some bad news for the owner on his or her return.

Monitor for appropriate language and report to the students on their performance.

## 12.13 Written work

Some possible beginnings:

1 Dear Sirs:
   Please find enclosed an ACME radio-cassette player which I bought two weeks ago. I have only used it a few times and now it won't work anymore. The main problem seems to be that . . .

2 Dear Sirs:

I have just come back from a two-week vacation in Honolulu with my club. We were on a package tour handled by your company. I am writing to you to complain about the hotel we stayed at, which was the Hotel Paradise. On our arrival at the hotel we were shocked to find that . . .

3 Dear Alan,

I was really upset to hear about your exams. I know you worked very hard in all your courses and really deserve to pass. I suppose it was a case of bad nerves – the kind we all suffer from before exams – but . . .

# 13 Describing places, describing people

## Functional objectives

Students will extend their ability to describe the appearances of buildings, cities, and other kinds of places and their attitudes to them, and to describe the appearance and character of people they know.

## 13.1    Conversation 🔊

The setting: Mary telephones her friend Sue to ask about Jim Wilson ...

Alternatively, describe to the class a place you know and someone who lives there or your own house and the members of your family. Encourage students to ask questions.

## 13.2    Presentation: describing places 🔊

Get the students to close their eyes for a moment and try to visualize the outside of the building you're in and the city you're in and the country-side around you. Encourage them to try to describe each in as much detail as possible and to ask for the words they need. Here are a few of the words they might need:

Building materials:
*concrete, brick, siding, stucco, wood shingles*

Streets:
*alley, wide avenue, intersection, freeway, interchange*

Countryside:
*woods, forests, family farms, commercial farms, orchards*

But this book cannot predict what they will need – only you and the class know that. So allow plenty of time for questions at all stages of this unit. Write the new and useful words on the blackboard and allow the class time to make notes.

Here and in 13.3 you could use a set of magazine (or calendar) pictures. These are best if glued onto large cards so that they can be shown to the class and passed around. Look together at some of the pictures in your set, and work out good descriptions.

## 13.3    Exercise as a class

Spend some time encouraging questions about each postcard. Perhaps start the ball rolling by demonstrating how the students might describe one of the scenes:

This is the famous Statue of Liberty that welcomes people to New York City and to America. The statue stands alone on a small island. In contrast, the skyscrapers in the background are crowded close together. Ships are going by in the river . . .

Show the class more of your pictures and work out a good description of each.

You could also do the following activity in small groups with your pictures or with smaller pictures on postcards or cut out of travel brochures and pasted onto cards:

Each student is given a card. The students should then describe their pictures without showing them to their partners. The partners should try to visualize the scenes being described, and they are allowed to ask questions.

## 13.4    Exercise in small groups

Perhaps demonstrate how to begin by describing a well-known building to the class and asking them to guess what it is (Empire State Building? Sears Tower?).

## 13.5    Exercise in groups of three or four

Again, you could give a glowing description of your favorite place first. Monitor each group and report to the whole class.

## 13.6    Presentation: describing people 🔲

The ideal starting point for this is another set of magazine pictures, pasted onto large cards (in collecting these, look for photos of people of different ages, in different moods and clothes – not just happy young fashion models). Alternatively, begin by looking at the people on the front cover of this book, or by thinking about absent friends or acquaintances.

Encourage the class to find out the words they need from each other, from you, or from the dictionary. For example, they might need some of these words:

General personal impression: *friendly, aggressive, attractive, cheerful*
Age: *thirtyish, in his or her early/mid-/late thirties, middle-aged, in his or her teens*
Height,* weight,* build, or figure: *tall and slim, athletic, well-built, overweight*
Face, hair, eyes, complexion, etc.: *oval face, curly hair, wavy hair, bushy eyebrows, Roman nose*

Clothes: *well-dressed, casual clothes, baggy pants, a loose jumper, sweater*
Character: *sensitive, generous, narrow-minded, excitable, level-headed*
Interests, sports, and hobbies: *enjoys sailing, spends a lot of time sewing*
Job: *lawyer, teacher, engineer*
Their life so far – achievements, family background, etc.: *well-qualified, an only child, eldest daughter, single*

Make sure your students realize that it is extremely rude to say to someone things like:

*You are narrow-minded.*
*You are overweight.*

Spend plenty of time during this presentation, and during the exercises that follow, answering questions from the students about words they need.

\* Metric equivalents of some typical heights and weights for students used to thinking metrically:

6 feet = 1.83 meters          (1 foot = 12 inches)
5 feet, 6 inches = 1.68 meters     (1 meter = 3 feet, 3 inches)
140 pounds = 63 kilos          (1 kilo = 2.2 pounds)
168 pounds = 76 kilos
210 pounds = 95 kilos

Note that heights are often given with the singular *foot*:
*She's about five-foot-six.*

---

## 13.7    *Exercise as a class*

Perhaps use the picture cards again. Make sure each student describes several people.
Correct mistakes and supply needed words.

---

## 13.8    *Exercise as a class*

Start the ball rolling by standing (or sitting) back-to-back with one student and describing him or her yourself. Then he or she describes you. Then let the first pair begin.
Supply needed words.

---

## 13.9    *Exercise in small groups*

After the groups have finished, perhaps ask students to describe to the class:

their old schoolteacher
their boss
a local character
the school bully at their first school (or their best friend)

## 13.10    *Consolidation exercise in groups of three or four*

Monitor each group and report to the class afterward. Ask each group to report their most vivid or interesting description to the class.

## 13.11    *Written work*

Some possible beginnings:

1 He's just over six feet tall and quite slim. He's got dark brown curly hair, which is quite long. He usually wears jeans and a sweater. He has brown eyes and a crooked nose. He's clean shaven. He always wears a silver identity bracelet on his right wrist . . .

2 All the houses look the same on Jackson Road. The one you want is about halfway down the road on the left. It has a natural wood front door. The front of the house is red brick, but if you look around at the right-hand side you'll see that it's dark brown siding. There's a small tree just outside the front door and . . .

3 One of the most irritating people I know is a man about my age who looks quite a bit older. He seems to be very friendly and wise. But if you talk to him for a while, you find out that he hasn't listened to what you've been saying at all. Take the other day, for example . . .

# 14 Telling a story: narrative techniques, handling dialogue, controlling a narrative

## Functional objectives

Students will extend their ability to sustain a narrative (as they tell the story of an interesting event or experience, an anecdote, or the plot of a novel, or movie) by creating some suspense, involving the listener, using appropriate opening and closing phrases, marking digressions, giving full quotations, or reporting the main points of what someone said.

## Presupposed knowledge

Students should already know:
— how to talk about past events, as practiced in unit 4
— the use of the past continuous (*was doing*) and past perfect (*had done*)
— methods of showing sequence of events (such as *Before ... After ...,* *As soon as ... , Not until ...* )
— the rules of reported, or indirect, speech (as in *He said that he was going to arrive at seven*)

---

### 14.1 Conversation

The setting: Anne tells her friend John about the time her big van got hit by a little Datsun truck in Texas ...

Alternatively, tell the class about an unforgettable experience of your own or an anecdote.

---

### 14.2 Presentation: narrrative techniques

Perhaps use the following story as a mechanical drill, getting different students to rephrase lines using the *What he did was* and *What happened was* structures:

*Crime doesn't pay?*

John had a fight with Bill.
Bill punched John on the nose.
John hit him back.
Bill fell out of the window.
And was killed.
John said to himself, "Oh my god!"
And started thinking what to do.

He looked around the room.
He saw Bill's wallet lying on the floor.
And he said, "Good god!"
He picked it up.
And looked inside and saw that it was full of $50 bills.
He counted them.
He said, "Twenty bills. That makes one thousand dollars."
He put the money in his own wallet.
He went to a travel agent.
And said, "First class one-way to Las Vegas, please."
He went to the airport.
The plane took him to Las Vegas.
He went straight to the casino.
He found a roulette table.
He said, "One thousand dollars on number seven, please."
Number seven came up.
He thought, "I'll try again."
Number seven came up again.
John became a wealthy man.
He returned to the airport.
He bought a ticket to South America.
The plane got him there safely.
He bought a luxury apartment.
He said to himself, "Poor old Bill."
He opened another bottle of champagne.

Point out that these structures cannot be used very often in a real narrative.

Ask about some other ways of involving the listener, such as:

*You may not believe this, but ...*
*You may find this hard to believe, but ...*
*Guess what – ...*

---

## 14.3    *Exercise as a class*

Point out that the so-called historical or narrative present tense is often used in telling stories. It is often used in comic strips, to describe the plots of movies or novels, and to tell anecdotes.

With the comic strip here, get the class to begin like this:

*A few weeks ago, Cathy went to eat at a restaurant.*
*She was alone ...*

Correct mistakes and advise the students how to tell the story in their own words – it may help to look at the story together first and then tell the story with books closed.

## 14.4 Communication activity in pairs

Student A: activity 135
Student B: activity 85
(An extra student can team up with A or B.)

Each student has a comic strip to put into his or her own words. Allow time for preparation.

Monitor the activity and encourage students to add detail and dialogue, and to say what happened before and after.

## 14.5 Exercise in groups

Possibly encourage the use of the present tense here:

*. . . so Michael gets back from the war and his friends throw a party to welcome him home. But he feels embarrassed and goes to a motel that evening and arrives home just as the party is ending . . .*

Monitor each group and give advice.

## 14.6 Presentation: handling dialogue

Perhaps record an interview from the radio, or two students role-playing an interview, or yourself being interviewed. Use the recording as a starting point for practicing reporting the main idea (or gist) or the actual words.

## 14.7 Communication activity in pairs

Student A: activity 46
Student B: activity 111
(An extra student can team up with A or B.)

This activity is in three stages:

1 Each student has a short passage that describes in reported speech what two people said about something. The student changes this to a dialogue containing the actual words of the speakers. This may need checking or correcting before the next stage.
2 Each student takes his or her partner's dialogue and rewrites it in reported form.
3 The rewritten reported text is compared with the original reported text in the partner's activity section.

Monitor the activity and help out if students are having difficulty. Discuss the differences between the three versions.

## 14.8    *Presentation: controlling a narrative*  🔲

Use the comic strip from 14.3 again or a comic strip of your own.

## 14.9    *Communication activity in pairs*

Student A: activity 140
Student B: activity 149
(An extra student can team up with B.)

Each student has a short story to tell to his or her partner. A has an adapted version of the James Thurber fable "The Little Girl and the Wolf," and B has a story about an ancient king. Make it clear to the students that they should try to "spin the story out" by adding detail and dialogue. Those who are listening should ask the narrator questions while the story is being told.

Monitor the activity and report your comments to the class afterward. Ask the students to suggest ways in which their storytelling could be improved.

## 14.10    *Exercise in small groups*

Perhaps get the ball rolling by telling the class about an experience you had, or a dream, or an anecdote.

Monitor each group and report on their performance at the end.

If your students seem confident enough, ask them all to prepare another story to tell in front of the whole class in the next lesson. Something that once happened to them or to a friend or relative might be a suitable topic.

## 14.11    *Consolidation exercise as a class*

In this game, students sit in a circle (or some other type of continuous chain). With an odd number of students, join the circle yourself. Every second student is an A, the others are Bs.
The first round begins with each A telling the B on the right a short experience, joke, or funny story. Each story keeps getting passed to the right, all the way around the circle and back to the A who first told it. The second round begins with the Bs each telling a story that gets passed around to the left.
After each round, ask everyone to report on how their story had changed by the time it got back to them.

## 14.12 *Written work*

Some possible beginnings:

1  Dear Caroline,
    You'll never believe this, but it really happened. I was sitting at home
    reading a book when the telephone rang. Well, I answered it and it
    was a voice I didn't recognize. The voice said . . .

2  ORDEAL OF HIJACK HOSTAGES
    The 150 passengers held hostage in the Boeing 747 hijacked at O'Hare
    Airport were released last night unharmed. They had been held prisoner
    for 72 hours without food. The hijackers had threatened to . . .
*and*
    We started our vacation three days late after a terrifying experience.
    Just as our plane was about to take off, an announcement came over
    the intercom to tell us that . . .

# 15 Dealing with moods and feelings: anger, sadness, indifference. Saying goodbye

## Functional objectives

Students will extend their ability to deal with people who are angry, sad, or indifferent and will learn to say goodbye in different ways.

---

**15.1**  *Conversation*

The setting: Mary Graham welcomes her husband home at the end of the day, but Bob is very grumpy . . .

Alternatively, you could storm into the classroom slamming the door and pretend to be angry first, then sad, then indifferent. Challenge your students to calm you down, cheer you up, and arouse your interest.
Or arrange for another teacher to come in "unexpectedly," pretending to be angry about something. Calm him or her down and then say how depressed you are about something else. When the other teacher has cheered you up, pretend to be indifferent about something else. Then say goodbye to each other as if you're parting for a very long time.

---

**15.2**  *Presentation: anger*

This section focuses on interpreting degrees of anger and on reacting to other people's anger. Students may also want to try showing anger themselves; however, keep in mind that in real life they are unlikely to want to get angry with other people in English and that if they do, they will probably lose the ensuing argument with a native speaker.

Ask for ideas on other ways to express annoyance:

*What a drag!*     *What a hassle!*
*What a pain!*     *What a nuisance!*

Point out that the tone of voice may be the only sign that someone is annoyed (or in a bad mood, or furious). Demonstrate this.

Ask for other swear words that the students have heard:

*Shit!*
*Christ!*
*God damn it!*

Point out that many people may be offended by "bad language." Students should avoid using swear words.

Ask for other ways of being furious:

*I can't stand the way he always . . .*
*This is the last straw . . .*

And ask for other ways of dealing with someone who is angry:

*Aw, come on – relax!*
*Hey, why don't you . . .*

## Additional work

Exercises 15.3 and 15.4 concentrate on calming down people who are angry. If your students want to spend a little time practicing having arguments or provoking people into getting angry, give them examples of some of the following surefire ways of antagonizing someone:

*Look here, you, . . .*
*You stupid idiot!*
*Listen here!*
*For god's sake, why don't you . . .*
*Don't be such an idiot!*

If your students agree that this kind of language might be worth practicing, divide them into two groups for an extra communication activity which isn't referred to in the Student Book. One group should look at activity 97 while the other one looks at activity 131. Each group begins by discussing the most annoying behavior of the other group. When they are ready, they can start criticizing each other. This can be done in pairs, small groups, or in the original large groups. (The group looking at activity 131 thinks the other group is too serious and humorless. The group looking at activity 97 thinks the other group is frivolous and lazy.)

WARNING: If there are people in your class who dislike each other or who might get upset, don't do this communication activity.

---

**15.3**    *Exercise*

If students need extra ideas, you could suggest an imaginary series of annoying things that have happened:

A teacher lost their homework.
They were late for school or work.
Their coffee was too cold to drink.
The weather is terrible.
Someone was rude to them.
etc.

Perhaps tell the class how you hate waiting in line and get them to calm you down.

## 15.4    *Communication activity in pairs*

Student A goes from activity 115 to 18 to 12 to 146 to 127 to 69
Student B goes from activity 42 to 130 to 118 to 113 to 88 to 76
(An extra student can join A or B.)

Each part of the activity has one student being angry and the other (a friend)
calming him or her down. The situations consist of being angry about:

an inconsiderate roommate called John
a friend called Jane who is never on time
an unsuccessful complaint in a shoe store
being questioned by a store detective
being involved in a minor bicycle accident
going to a restaurant (which the partner is
 thought to have recommended, but in fact didn't)

## 15.5    *Presentation: sadness*

Demonstrate and practice by telling the class some of your own
imaginary problems and getting them to cheer you up:

Your children are sick.
Your grandmother died.
You lost your watch.
You had a fight with your best friend.
Your wife or husband has just left you.
etc.

## 15.6    *Communication activity in pairs*

Student A: part one – activity 103      part two – activity 152
Student B: part one – activity 59      part two – activity 66
(An extra student can team up with A or B.)

First student B has a list of disasters that have happened to him or her, and
student A has to cheer B up. Then, when B is happier, A is depressed and
has to be cheered up.

Monitor the activity and offer sympathetic advice.

## 15.7    *Communication activity in pairs*

Student A goes from activity 121 to 37 to 24 to 139 to 125
Student B goes from activity 49 to 28 to 68 to 78 to 15
(An extra student can team up with you.)

In part one, A has a problem, B is cheerful.
In part two, B has a problem, A is cheerful.
In part three, A has a problem, B is cheerful.
And so on.

The sad partner must be cheered up before the pair can look at the next
activity.

## 15.8 Presentation: indifference 🔲

Perhaps demonstrate and practice by showing indifference while the students tell you about their hobbies. Have them try to get you interested.

Point out and demonstrate that indifference is often only expressed by the tone of voice:

*Oh yeah?*
*I see.*
*Very nice.*
*Interesting.*

## 15.9 Communication activity in pairs

Student A goes from activity 153 to 147
Student B goes from activity 55 to 122
(An extra student can join A or B.)

A begins by being indifferent to B's ideas and then B pretends to be indifferent to A's ideas.

## 15.10 Consolidation exercise as a class: moods and feelings

Begin by dividing the class into four groups: Group A will be feeling angry, group B depressed, group C indifferent, and group D happy. After each group has gotten together by itself and established its mood, get everyone to stand up and talk to different people from other groups trying to influence them to share their mood.

At the end, find out what happened. Were they able to change anyone else's mood?

## 15.11 Presentation: saying goodbye 🔲

Ask for other ideas on saying goodbye informally when you are meeting again soon:

*See you later!*
*See you soon!*
*Bye now!*

(Perhaps point out that *Bye-bye* sometimes sounds a little childish and that in more formal situations you can say *Goodbye!* or, at the end of a day's work, *Good night!*)

Ask for other ideas on saying goodbye for a long time:

*I hope everything goes well.*
*Take care now, you hear!*
*Let's hope it's au revoir.*

## 15.12  *Exercise as a class*

Everyone has to say goodbye to everyone else in the room, pretending that this is their last meeting.

## 15.13  *Communication activity*

Everyone looks at activity 45, which says goodbye to them.

## 15.14  *Written work*

Begin by discussing the topic – the class's comments will be useful for you the next time you use *Functions of American English*.